LIFE'S STEERING WHEEL

BY

PAUL WAYNE MORRIS

To my loving wife Linda, for her encouragement, patience and help
in the preparation of this undertaking.
To Arden Dorney, who inspired my writing through his friendship
and constant encouragement.
I also wish to dedicate this writing to my daughters, Shannon
Wood, and Sharra Morris, my son-in-law, Chris Wood, and my two
wonderful grandsons, Connor Wood and Nathan Wood.

This is for you.

CONTENTS

PHOTOS

Black Sunday
Dirty 30s
The Mauldins
John H. Johnson
Roscoe and Paul
Paul, David, Roscoe
Paul and His Pig
Linda and Paul's Wedding
Shannon and Linda
Calvin Vanzandt
Paul and Linda
Roscoe and Ernest
Richard Carmichael and Family
Shawn Laughlin and Tim Scott
Peggy and George Roach
Linda and Paul
Nathan and Connor Wood
Joan Morris
District V
My Girls
Shannon, Chris, Nathan, Connor Wood
Chris and Shannon Wood
Chris Frech, Terry Jantz, Patty Lanier, Ed Wrather, Jerry Graybill
Oil Boom
Sharra and Paul
First Car
Paul and Linda 2006 Cruise
Patty and Bob Lanier and Daughters
Sharra, Shannon, Paul
President Carter
Paul and Linda at Retirement

LIFE'S STEERING WHEEL

OCINA

Oklahoma is known for many things. It is said to be the home of the "Red man," part of "tornado alley," and in the 1930s, shared with other plains states the distinction of being a major contributor to the "Dust Bowl," sometimes referred to as the "Dirty Thirties."

It was also during the time of the Great Depression (1929-1939) thought by many to have been caused by the crash of the stock market. Democrats blamed the Republicans and they responded by casting the blame back. Others would say, God was punishing people for their sins. The reasons for hard economic times would be debated for years, but there was not one single cause. Hard times were not confined to the borders of the United States as the Great Depression proved to be a worldwide calamity.

Because of a severe drought and poor land management practices by farmers, the plains states were all but decimated by the gigantic rolling clouds of top soil pushed across the land. It is estimated that the "Dust Bowl" played a significant part in lengthening the effects of the Great Depression.

It has been said, that many people lost their minds during those trying times. It was impossible to escape the fine dust particles invading even the tightest structures. The dirty brown film covered everything: dishes, clothing and furniture. Nothing was exempt. Families draped wet bed sheets over windows and doors, stuffed every crack they could find, wore damp cloths over their faces, but there was no escaping the brown evil covering the land.

In many locations across the plains, the swirling, rolling storms of dust drifted much like snow. Fences, farm implements and even many barns and houses gave in to the waves of dust and were partially or completely covered over.

8

On April 14, 1935, people in the plains states witnessed one of the most devastating dust storms. The day began as a bright clear morning with many people out of their homes attending church services and enjoying the sunshine. By mid-afternoon, the massive cloud of dust could be seen on the horizon. Many people hurried to return home ahead of the storm, while others were caught on the roads, forced to seek shelter in abandoned buildings or other places of refuge. Some people became victims in their own yards, unable to find their way into their homes. Many thought it was the end of the world. That day would later be labeled as "Black Sunday." It was little wonder many families loaded whatever their vehicles could carry and left everything else behind.

From 300,000 to 400,000 people were displaced as a result of these tragedies, as families were uprooted and cast in all directions. As John Steinbeck wrote in his 1939 novel, The Grapes of Wrath: "And then the dispossessed were drawn west - from Kansas, Oklahoma, Texas, New Mexico; from Nevada and Arkansas, families, tribes, dusted out, tractored out. Car-loads, caravans, homeless and hungry; twenty thousand and fifty thousand and a hundred thousand and two hundred thousand. They streamed over the mountains, hungry and restless – restless as ants, scurrying to find work to do – to lift, to push, to pull, to pick, to cut – anything, any burden to bear, for food. The kids are hungry. We got no place to live. Like ants scurrying for work, for food, and most of all for land."

The countless thousands, who left their farms and homes in search of a better life, migrated in a myriad of directions. People were displaced to where they had family members, while a great numbers were drawn to the state of California, where it was reported workers were needed. Migrant work was available in that state, but not to the extent to accommodate the swelling influx of the poor and hungry. As a result, California law enforcement officers were sent to the borders with instructions to turn back those families who had no money. That practice, however, did not last and the great migration to California continued to the extend that the news media labeled many of them as "Okies." It did not seem to matter that many were from other states.

There is an old saying in the Sooner State: "If you don't like the weather, just hang around awhile." It is not uncommon to see rain in the morning, a sandstorm at mid-day and snow and sleet the same night. "Predicting the weather in this part of the world has made more liars than the game of golf." – a quote from Mark Twain.

As I age, recalling the extreme fluctuations in the climate has become more difficult. In fact, at 65, remembering anything from my past causes lengthy gaps in my speech, blank stares and severe headaches. Mark Twain said: "When I was younger, I could remember anything, whether it had happened or not; but my faculties are decaying now and soon I shall be so I cannot remember any but the things that never happened." The great humorist certainly had a command of the English language, but memories, as patchwork in a quilt, binds together the very essence of who we are. Can you imagine going through life without the ability to go back in time by using your mind? Recalling those bad experiences aids us in avoiding the same mistakes over and over, while good memories help us through bad times. And yes, there will always be those who continually make the same blunders, learning little from their mistakes. Those individuals overload our courts and cause our taxes to increase year after year as the dysfunctional family cycle continues.

My first childhood memories are as a five-year-old boy living with my family near Ocina, Oklahoma. Dead center in "tornado alley" in the rural southwest area of the state, the weather was always diverse, for lack of a better explanation.

The days of the "Dust Bowl" had ended, with farmers more aware of conservation. Shelterbelts were set in place, cover crops planted and crop rotation was implemented. The Federal Government began to play a more active role in agricultural affairs in an attempt to divert another catastrophe. World War II had come to a close, with many families returning to life on the farm. The economy was beginning to heal.

As with many Southwest Oklahoma communities during the 1940s, several farm families lived on a section of land (640 acres) carving out a meager existence for, what we would consider today, large families. The concept was: the more children, the more workers.

My Father, Roscoe Franklin Morris, was the third child born to Laburr and Leola Bell (Mauldin) Morris, who were married December 28, 1906, in Habersham County Georgia. The following children were born to that union: Reginald Burns Morris, born February 5, 1908, Seneca, South Carolina; Firzell F. Morris, born March 4, 1908, Seneca, South Carolina; Roscoe Franklin Morris, born May 22, 1912, Honea Path, South Carolina; Nellie Mae Morris, born September 30, 1913, in Oconee County, South Carolina; Iceland Estelle Morris, born March 31, 1915, Walhalla, South Carolina. The family moved to Southwest Oklahoma when my Father was in his teens. I believe the move was, primarily, due to the availability of farmland, but there may have been other reasons I am not aware of.

The Morris and Mauldin families have deep roots in the Habersham County, Georgia area. Both my grandparents - my Father's side of the family - were reared in the "hill country" in northeast Georgia and South Carolina. The families could truly be labeled as "mountain people" living in log cabins, existing off the land. In those days, the cabin doors were open most of the time with no screens on the windows. Families raised corn, cabbage, beans and all kinds of vegetables in the summer time, but had no way of preserving food for winter. Instead of canning, they made hominy, kraut and dried apples that grew wild in the mountains. Their meat consisted of wild hogs and other wild game.

I'm not sure what the Mauldin Family was thinking when they gave names to my great uncles. Their names were: Raught, Ruff, Tuff, and Taught. When my brother and I had difficulty remembering their names, Dad told us to remember them in this manner: Raught Taught Ruff to be Tuff. That worked.

My grandmother was the first to leave the mountains. She was unhappy with the way her family lived, so she moved to Clarksville,

Georgia where she lived with an aunt. She began working in the cotton mills to earn a living. When my grandfather was old enough, he also began to work in the mills. That was where my grandparents met and started dating, although they had known each other most of their life.

Laburr and Leola Bell Morris purchased thirteen acres of land before the war, affording them a good standard of living. After the war, they mortgaged their farm in order to purchase another thirteen-acre plot which joined their original farm. In 1924, the boll weevils hit the cotton, causing their crops not to produce enough to pay the mortgage. With financial problems on the horizon, as well as the realization of losing their land, they moved to Southwest Oklahoma where the Mauldin Family had settled.

I will share an interesting family story with you. Jincy Josephine Morris was the first cousin of my great grandfather. When it was time for her to give birth, a neighbor, Mrs. Dempsey, who was a midwife, delivered the child. Two years after her child was born, she delivered Mrs. Dempsey's child, William Harrison Dempsey. He was also known as Jack Dempsey who later became boxing Heavyweight Champion of the world.

My Mother's parents, John H. and Alpha (Lawson) Johnson, were married at Baloon, Arkansas in 1903. In 1912, they sold their farm near Plainview, Arkansas, loaded their possessions in a covered wagon and headed for Oklahoma. They had two daughters at that time: Myrtle, age eight, and Winnie, age six. A pair of young mules pulled the wagon. In 1916, they purchased a farm south of Moravia, in Greer County, Oklahoma. In 1923, John, better known as "Shorty" built the first Ocina Store and Blacksmith Shop east of the school. By that time, they had added two additional daughters to the family: Joan and Lois.

My Mother, Gladys Louisa Sally Joan Johnson, born May 19, 1915, at Granite, Oklahoma, met and married my Father, December 8, 1933, in Sayre, Oklahoma. The somewhat strange name given to my Mother, has always been an embarrassment to her, but a great source of humor to the rest of her family. She attempted to explain the multiple names by saying, "All the rest of the kids had a shot at naming me." Apparently, her parents simply adopted all the names. She only used the name, Joan.

My Father farmed 160 acres of sandy land, (owned by his father-in-law, J. H. "Shorty" Johnson) was a school custodian and bus driver at Ocina School. The school was located on the Beckham and Greer County line with all school buildings on the south side of the road in Greer County. In addition to the school income, my parents sold cream and eggs to a local produce store in Willow, Oklahoma. That small but lively little town was only four miles from our home.

Several things stand out in my mind about my Mother's father, but the fact that he had a glass eye seemed to spark the interest of a young boy. According to my Mother, he lost his eye while driving cattle through a mesquite pasture. I'm sure some of the family talked him into being fitted with the prostheses, but he was never particularly taken with it, often scraping on it with a pocket knife attempting a better fit. From what I have been told, he was driving down the road one day and simply threw it out the window.

He was also known to be a shrewd trader, especially when it came to horses, cattle and wolf hounds. It was said, "If you trade with Shorty, you'd better count your fingers after shaking on the deal." Father said, "He's got the first dollar he ever made in the bank drawing interest."

Our old house had been built on a foundation of limestone rocks, affording local "critters" a cool place to escape the summer heat. An occasional skunk made life somewhat difficult but interesting. At only five years old, I thought the house had been built by early settlers (real early) or perhaps, Indians who had not mastered the art of building, and simply threw some wood in a pile. Paint would have accomplished little, as the boards covering the outside were weathered beyond description. I recall pushing on the inside wall of the living room with enough force to see the bare ground under the house.

My brother and I shared a bedroom which had been added to

the south side of the house. When it rained, we could not sleep because of the noise on the sheet-metal roof. With all its problems, I can still remember the good times there, and some of the bad.

As we call to mind things from our childhood, I think most of my memories are, at the least, strange. I seem to remember sounds rather than events, or at least some sounds. I can still identify the sound (at least in my mind) made by the tightly wound Sunday newspaper as it dropped to the ground, having been thrown from a small airplane. Families who were fortunate enough to afford such a luxury, were identified from the air by a white circle painted on the roof of the house. There are some things we never forget. I remember how disappointed my brother and I were when the pilot of the small aircraft made a poor toss. One of several Locust trees around our house was occasionally the recipient of the paper. By the time the tightly rolled paper hit the ground, it was no more than confetti. We always made some attempt to salvage the cartoons but were rarely successful. My Father seldom failed to mention how thankful we should be that the paper didn't hit the house. That was little consolation for two small boys waiting for the "funnies".

Several years later, I had the opportunity to talk with a man who had "thrown" the Sunday paper from an airplane. He told about an old gentleman who was always trying to catch the paper. The man said he always watched and threw the paper away from the old man so he could not catch it. One morning the pilot was late and was trying to make up time on his route. He flew over the old man's house and simply tossed the paper without looking. The old gentleman finally realized his life long dream; he caught the Sunday paper. He now had a broken shoulder, arm and several ribs. The pilot landed and took the old man to the hospital.

That also brings back memories, not only of the falling paper, but how a small boy thinks. I could envision the heavy Sunday paper crashing through the roof causing extensive damage to our house. I also thought about the paper falling on my older brother, David (four years my senior) causing instant death. I had those illusions at various times, but more so when he failed to treat his younger brother fairly, with the respect he deserved. It is very fortunate that God does not grant all the prayers of a five-year-old.

As most farm families of the 1940s, we had not yet caught up with the latest craze - indoor plumbing. Our "outhouse" was about 30 yards from the front door. At the time, the distance seemed much farther (something around a mile in the summertime and two miles during the winter months). The fear factor also played a part in the variable distance, and with an older brother, there was no end to stories of grotesque monsters, aliens from Mars, vicious killers of small boys, blood suckers and any assortment of winged creatures preying exclusively on five-year-olds, especially at night. I was convinced evil beasts "staked out" the route to the outdoor toilet eagerly waiting for their next (short) victim.

Making a safe trek to the privy then back to the front door, was always due to several heart-felt petitions to God. I could never understand why God continually granted my prayers concerning the privy but never the deathblow to my brother, brought on by the Sunday paper. Perhaps, He knew we did not have the resources to repair the roof.

Our water source was also several yards from the house. The windmill, in addition to supplying fresh water for our cattle and other animals, provided for our daily needs. But, someone had to walk to the windmill with a large bucket, fill it with water then return to the house. At five years old and small, I usually escaped that delegated chore. My brother, who often carried out the duty, never failed to remind me, "You will always be little, and as you get older, your legs will get shorter until you simply disappear at about the age of seven." I never really believed him, because I knew other boys who were about that age, and their legs never seemed to get shorter. Never-the-less, he explained this unholy phenomena often enough to cause great concern on my part. Would God never answer my prayers in regard to the Sunday paper? Dad could simply nail tin over the hole in the roof; it would not require extensive repair. I often explained that to God, as I begged for some measure of "brotherly" relief. Of course there were times when my brother would come to my aid when a bully persecuted me. At those times, I would amend my prayers to having the falling newspaper merely cripple David. After all, one never knew when a bully would surface, requiring some measure of retribution from my brother.

My parents, thoughtfully, brought only the two of us into the world. I'm sure their decision was based solely on careful observation of their two "boys" as they attempted to exterminate each other. If there was any meanness or mayhem we failed to create, it could not be described. Whether it was "knocking" each other in the head with a brick or garden hoe, or beating each other's face in, we were constantly creating visions of a childless family to our parents. I know this to be true because they carefully explained it to us often. They told us, "We brought you into the world and we can take you out, then make another one just like you." I never really understood that concept, because they also told us there could never be two more boys like us.

No doubt they understood the penalties for murder, otherwise, David and I would not be alive today.

Of course you must understand, there was little to keep a young boy out of trouble in those days. We played on the sandy hills of our farm, with neighboring children, but what we waited for with great anticipation, were the trips to Elk City with our Father. Those cherished excursions usually occurred every two or three months when a calf was sold at the cattle auction. My brother and I were allowed to trade comic books at a small secondhand store while waiting for the sale to end. If things went well at the auction, we were sometimes rewarded with a small toy or other surprise. One such toy I will remember forever was a water pistol for each of us. We talked Father into stopping outside Elk City which allowed us time to shoot each other for a few minutes.

At night, we could hardly wait for our favorite radio programs. With no electricity in our home, we were fortunate to have a wind charger near the windmill, which powered our Philco Radio in the living room. Some of the programs I remember were: The Shadow, The Lone Ranger, Fibber McGee and Molly, The Squeaking Door, The Green Hornet, Lum and Abner, Dagwood and Blondie, Amos N Andy, The Great Gildersleeve, Life With Luigi and the Red Skelton Show. I think my favorites were The Shadow and The Lone Ranger. The introduction music to those programs always caused chill bumps. I was continually amazed by the Lone Ranger's uncanny ability to know what the bad guys were going to do next. They were no match for Tonto and The Lone Ranger as they were always one step ahead of the villains. If the wind did not power the wind charger and battery for the radio, it was a sad time for the entire family. I think my parents enjoyed those times as much as my brother and I. Keeping up with the radio programs was about the only recreation for all of us in the evenings.

I believe kids today would simply die of boredom if required to live as we did in the late 1940s. There were no cell phones, ipods, computers, televisions, Playstations, X-boxes, Internet, hand-held electronic games or other battery powered gadgets. We could not hang out at the mall, soda shop or drive-in, but if those luxuries had been available, we certainly had no money.

In the summertime, we left the house in the morning and didn't return until just before sunset. Being outside most of the time meant relying solely on the companionship of our friends. With so many families farming in relatively close proximity, it was only a short distance in any direction to many of our friends and we certainly didn't mind walking. We played a great deal of the time at the east boundary of our land where there was a railroad track. We learned very quickly that a penny carefully placed on the track would become a "quarter-sized penny" once the train passed over it.

If the railroad does not seem the safe or proper setting for young boys, you may be correct. However, I don't think parents worried so much about their children in those days. We were "self sufficient" in the entertainment realm, but more importantly, we were adept at caring for ourselves. We fell out of trees, broke bones and teeth, yet there were no lawsuits. Our cabinets or medicine bottles did not have child-proof locks, yet we seemed to survive. We drank out of the same containers with no thoughts of germs. We imagined, invented and made most of our games and toys, giving us a greater appreciation of life in general. Most of the things we played with were made from old tin cans, sticks, twine and baling wire. We might spend hours building something from those everyday items only to have them break down. Living with disappointment did not discourage us from continuing our day-to-day lives; there was no boredom to slow us down. It is my belief that young people of those times were more in tune with nature because it was so much a part of their lives.

Mother's cousin, P. C. and Mattie Johnson, lived just across the road from our house. Their son Bill was the same age as my brother, so they played together most of the time, usually excluding me because of my age. My closest friend was Anita Moore, who lived only a quarter-mile south. We spent countless hours in the forks of a large tree near our house discussing life's advantages and disadvantages or whatever young people of those times talked about.

Luther Bell and his family lived about a half-mile south of our house. David and I played with their boys (Dwight and Doyle) on occasion, but because of conflicts between our Fathers, we stayed away from their place most of the time.

The disagreement between Luther and my Dad occurred over some of their hogs coming over on our farm, then tearing down feed shocks. If you are not familiar with that term, I will explain. I suppose another name could be bundle-feed. Maze or Milo was grown, cut and bundled (tied with twine) then stacked into something similar to an Indian's tepee. In the winter months, this was used to feed our cattle.

According to stories I have been told over the years, Dad did not ask Luther to pay for any damages; he merely asked him to keep his hogs out of our field. Sometime later, some of our calves got out and later wandered over on Luther's place. I don't know if they damaged anything on his farm, but he rounded them up and put them in a pen near his house. He then came to our house and asked Dad to reimburse him for crop damage. From what I have been told, he and Father entered into a heated argument with Luther walking backward across the yard with Dad's finger in his face. Luther tripped over something in the yard and fell. When he left, he returned home, let our calves out of the pen and instructed his boys to drive them back to our place. We pretty much kept our distance after that.

Lonzo and Lois Henderson lived less than a mile south from our place. Lois was my aunt (Mother's younger sister). I was always very close to their children, Jerry Don and Carolyn, with many hours spent walking back and forth from our house to theirs. In fact, Jerry Don and I managed to get into lots of trouble together. One instance that comes to mind was the time we drove about two dozen nails in my brother's bicycle tires while he was in school. I don't recall why we did such a thing; probably because we didn't have bicycles.

Most of us can remember at least some of the animals that have been a part of our lives. Certainly, living on a farm produced more opportunities to be around animals and to better understand them. When I was about five years old, my pet was a Poland China Hog. I think it must have weighed about 300 pounds, because I could barely see over its back. I don't remember if I properly named the animal and don't recall exactly what happened to it, but I have a good idea. Enough said about the pet pig.

My Father usually kept a few goats around the house (I still can't imagine why). One morning while we were all sitting around the kitchen table, my Dad jumped to his feet and ran to the back door. Naturally and with great interest, we all followed. We were all in shock when we saw what he was staring at. One of the goats was standing atop our Ford Model-A Touring car – better known as a "cloth-top." The (soon-to-be-deceased) goat was leisurely munching away at the "cloth-top" staring out across the field as if its actions were a normal, morning activity. It was very obvious that a great deal of the top was now missing, having been transformed into "goat food." Father reached for his Remington, .22-caliber rifle that was always leaning in the corner near the back door. I watched him pull the action back as he opened the screen door, taking dead aim in the goats direction. As the rifle fired, the old goat toppled to the ground with a piece of cloth hanging precariously from its mouth. There was little need to check for vital signs; we all knew he never missed. No one said a word. We simply returned to the kitchen table and finished eating. I can't remember whether we butchered the goat, but I doubt that Father wanted further contact with the animal. I don't think he added to his "goat operation" after that incident.

Ocina School was initially built in 1920 as a result of consolidation of three other small school districts in Greer County: Urbana, Ozoma and Chalk Bluff. Spring Creek and Laura Moore Schools later consolidated with Ocina. The two-story structure consisted of six rooms and a large auditorium, which could also be used for community meetings. The school was open for business the school year of 1920-1921. Ocina boasted of having the finest play-ground in the country, with a merry-go-round, swings, horizontal bars, see-saws and two outdoor basketball courts - The boys on one and the girls on the other.

In 1941, the school was remodeled, bringing the total number of classrooms to 14. In 1942, Willow High School was transferred to Ocina.

It is now 1948 and time that I made a formal appearance. I awoke one morning to discover my Mother and Father had enrolled me in the first grade. I did not remember discussing my need for an education, after all, what did playing day after day have to do with education? They said the time was right for my first attempt at education.

At age five, I was in the first grade at Ocina School. Where did all that time go? Yesterday I was frolicking about on the sand hills of our farm, then, suddenly, life changed.

My brother had been going to school for four years and although I was having the time of my life without him under my feet, my Mother and Father were sending me off to the same school. It simply did not seem fair, but what did I know.

I only attended the first grade at Ocina before our family relocated to the Lake Creek community, about ten miles east of Ocina. I'm sure my failure to recall that first school experience with any great detail, hinges on my complete lack of interest. I do recall that my teacher's name was Ms. Penn. What I remember most about her was the ability she possessed to look in two directions at the same time. Oh, and her hair, as my wife's uncle would say, "looks like she smelled a wolf." That must have been before hair salons. I don't remember if I passed the first grade under Ms Penn; I'm not sure she knew I was in her class.

The last graduating class at Ocina School was in 1957. With a declining population in the county, Ocina School District split in 1958, closed its doors and transferred students to Granite, Sayre and Carter. It is difficult to imagine, but in 1910, there were as many as 52 school districts in Greer County.

Mangum	Granite	Templeton
Headquarters	Quartz	Annie Laurie
Bloomington	Corinth	Russell Valley
Temple	City View	Midway /Willow
Miller Flat	Gyp Hill	Reed
Deer Creek	Hopewell	Harmony
Z.V./Ladessa	Marie	Hackberry
Prosperity	Plainview	New Hope
Haystack	Fairview	Elm Valley
Sand Hill	Wild Cat	Emmett
Shiloh	Ozona	McKissach
Laura Moore	Dean	Thompson
Redtop	Spring Branch	Yellow Canyon
Orient	Jaybuckle	Brake
Eagan	Oak Grove	Hal Smith
Valley View	Steen	Lowder
White Flat	Blake	

Because of the move toward urbanization, consolidating school districts would continue for several years. Small farm operations have continued to disappear at an alarming rate and as of 2007, there are only two school districts in Greer County - Granite and Mangum.

Lake Creek

My family moved to the Lake Creek Community in 1949. Some time before we relocated, my Father purchased the surface rights to 160 acres of school land approximately four miles northwest of Lake Creek. The State of Oklahoma owns several thousand acres of school land, which is rented to farmers on an annual basis. The revenue is used as support for local school districts.

In addition to the school land, my Father purchased 80 acres of land nearby. He bought a two-story house south of Lake Creek from Sam Russell and had it moved to our property. Dad made repairs on the house for several months before we moved from Ocina.

House-movers in those days did not possess sophisticated equipment as they do now, so, my Father made several repairs on the house following the move. In addition to the needed structural repairs, he built a bathroom onto the southeast side of the house. We also had the convenience of electricity. All this was completed before we relocated.

In a small boy's mind, things often appear much larger than they really are. The move to Lake Creek was certainly one of those times, as well as being a life-altering experience. It was as though I had stepped into another world.

The house was a gigantic, two-story, three-bedroom house that was larger than anything I had ever seen. The attic had more room than our old house at Ocina. I was positive the structure was larger than all the castles in all foreign countries. Every room of the house was huge with nine and ten-foot ceilings. But the size was not the only thing that amazed a small boy; we now had running water and did not have to leave the house to use the bathroom. It seemed odd to take a bath in a real bathtub.

We would continue to heat our new home by burning wood and coal in an old pot-bellied stove for a short time before having access to propane/butane. It was truly an amazing thing to behold and one that made a life-long impression on a six-year-old boy.

Our new home was located about 100 yards off the main county (dirt) road. Locust and Cottonwood trees by the hundreds struggled for sunlight because they were so dense. The thick shade provided in the summertime almost hid the house from the road. The narrow, sandy road leading from the main road to the front of our house, was covered by a canopy of tree limbs and leaves. The heavy foliage took on the appearance of a long tunnel making it almost impossible to see the sky when walking along this road.

My brother and I thought we had died and gone to heaven. We would continue to explore this "new world" for several months. We tirelessly searched this new "forest" constructing impenetrable forts and secret places that would keep us safe from Indians or any unknown dangers. We dug caves, built tree-houses and other structures, had ropes swinging from tree limbs, and blazed numerous trails. I remember the feelings I experienced when we moved into our new home; I felt like the lead character in a fairy tale.

The Lake Creek community consisted of numerous farm families scattered over several square miles in northeast Greer County. The central location of the community was the Lake Creek School, located about four miles southeast of our home. Along with the school, there was a grocery store and service station, a Baptist Church and Church of Christ. A cotton gin, operated by Sam Russell, was located east of the school, with a mechanic's shop just to the south, across the road. There were several dwellings in and around the school and store. Most of the people living there were somehow connected to the school, store, or one of the churches.

I think the Lake Creek store (approximately 200 yards south of the school) was the glue that held the community together. The O.K. Burkhalter family owned and operated the store and service station. It was more than a place to purchase food items for families or snacks for hungry school kids; it was a place to hang out and find out what was going on.

The store purchased chickens, eggs and cream from farm families and seemed to always have whatever was needed whether it was a fan belt, bag of flour, nuts and bolts or feed for livestock. They also sold school supplies, tires, tubes, auto accessories, butane, gasoline, kerosene and numerous brands of motor oil.

There was a candling table where eggs were examined before being purchased by the store. The store was always in some stage of expansion, building storage areas for a larger stock of goods. I could never understand how Mr. Burkhalter could always stock everything a person wanted or needed. He certainly had his finger on the pulse of the community. If the Lake Creek store didn't have it, you didn't need it.

My Father continued to drive a school bus for the school, as he had done for the school at Ocina. It seemed everyone had to supplement their income on the farm in some way. Times were hard.

Dad always brought the leftover food (we always referred to it as "slop") home from the school. In those days, when kids finished eating in the school lunch room, they were required to dump their trays in a large vat before stacking them and leaving. That was what our hogs ate.

Dad was constantly taking silverware back to the lunch room. It seemed some kids found it quicker to dump everything from their tray, including knives, forks and spoons. Although I can't recall if I was one of those students or not; I don't think my brother and I would have ever thrown away perfectly good eating utensils. After all, we, like most other people in the community, had very little. We never seemed to realize our state of affluence. Thinking back, I don't think we were ever without shoes, clothing or food. What else could we have wanted.

Lake Creek school was an excellent learning institution, with tennis, baseball, basketball, softball, track, 4H Club, FFA, debating teams, speaking contests, literary society, school plays and the school newspaper – The Bison.

I was in school again. The second grade. Where had the time gone? Although I recall very little of those early years, I do think I was involved in more than my share of meanness. I always attributed those "mean years" to my brother's poor example, but I no longer can take that stance. I was just mean all on my own; a poor example was just "icing on the cake."

My later grade-school years were checkered with such incidents as removing doors from their hinges, putting grass burs (commonly known as sandburs) in the teacher's chair, snakes in her desk and whatever I could think of to torment someone.

I remember taking an anti-personnel explosive to school. I had carefully placed a cherry bomb (outlawed now in the state of Oklahoma, with good reason – they will take off a finger) in a baseball-sized gourd, covering the outside with paraffin, then rolled it in gravel. Does that sound like a childish prank? I doubt that our military forces of those days had a more lethal weapon in their arsenal.

I checked the boys restroom to verify no students were inside before unleashing my "bomb." Somehow, I overlooked the fact that one of my (former) good friends, had darted into the restroom without being detected. At least that is my story and I'm sticking to it. I lit the short fuse and tossed it over a short wooden wing into the boys restroom. It made a lot of noise, covering the inside of the restroom with deadly flying gravel. What I then discovered was that James Lantz (as I said, a former good friend) was standing at the sink washing his hands, when the deadly projectile found its way into the back pocket of his Roundhouse Overalls. I did hear a strange muffled explosion, unlike most of my previous attempts as an explosive expert. James ran from the restroom screaming, holding his backside, all the while, leaving a trail of smoke and a strong smell of gun powder. I know that he still bears the scars from his encounter with my doomsday explosive.

The superintendent always managed to appear out of thin air when he was not needed; this was another of those appearances. He almost beat me to death with his belt and short piece of rope. My punishment was light, however, compared to James' affliction. And to make it even worse, that was not even close to some of my more interesting adventures. I think I received another beating when I returned home that day. I deserved both and more.

James and his family moved from Lake Creek shortly after my failed experiment. I always wondered if they left thinking I would sooner or later kill James. I don't think that was the reason. Mr. Lantz, James' father, was the school custodian. They left the community and moved to Shamrock, Texas. I believe they had family there.

James would later finish high school in Texas, marry and work many years for a natural gas company in that state. A few years ago, he retired and moved his family back to Oklahoma. In fact, he lives only a couple of blocks from me in Granite. We are still friends, although he narrows his eyes, conjures up strange facial features and sometimes takes a step backward when we see each other. I don't think I would have killed him if the family had remained at Lake Creek; It's hard to say. What do you think?

Some of my closest friends and constant companions at Lake Creek, were Jimmy and Tony McGee. They lived a couple of miles northwest of our place and their father farmed, as did most of the people in the community.

What I remember most about our exciting adventures, was the old white horse they rode. It reminded me of the Budweiser Clydesdales – the large feathered-legged draft horse. Its hooves were as large as the top of a galvanized, gallon bucket, but more importantly, that old horse had no fear. You could look him directly in the eyes, and you immediately knew; he was one of us. Whatever we prodded him to do, he obliged and, he was a jumper. I think he would have jumped off the edge of the world for us.

We spent countless hours on a nearby river jumping the old horse off cliffs and bluffs into water holes. Sometimes, it took a long time for the horse (and rider) to surface, but we were like the horse; we had no fear. Or perhaps I should say, we had no sense. It's a good thing our parents never knew what we were doing. And then, there was the old two-wheeled cart the boys pulled behind the horse. I can't count the times we wrecked it or turned it over. We also tried to set the land-speed record with a bicycle tied on behind old "Whitie." It would travel plenty fast until the front wheel started to wobble on those sandy roads, then we braced for a 25 or 30-mph crash. Did I mention that old "Whitie" was fast? Well, he was. And, he would laugh at us when we "bit the dust." Yes, he could laugh, of course in horse language. I don't recall ever being around a more intelligent animal. I can still visualize him standing over us (after a particularly bad spill) shaking his head, whinnying and pawing at the ground. We all knew he was laughing at us, so we just laughed back.

After all these years, I still think of that old horse and the unusual character he possessed. He would not have hesitated an instant if required to lead a charge into the face of overwhelming odds. What a horse.

We were also regulars at the river bridge between Willow and Carter. Just south of the river bridge, there was another crossing with a smaller bridge. The water hole below was spring fed and deep enough to dive into, head first.

Our usual contest was to strip off all our clothes, stand on the bridge rail waiting for a car. The last one into the water was the winner. I was a regular winner, sometimes not diving until the car had passed over the bridge. I don't know why I was so shameless, perhaps I didn't think anyone could see my tiny butt; I don't know.

It was fun while it lasted, until some passerby told my Father and Mother, then the naked diving contest came to a halt. I guess someone did see my tiny butt.

Some of my other friends were the Norman boys: John, Lewis, and Lynn. They also lived only a couple of miles away, which was no obstacle to a true adventurer. Oh, they also had a couple of sisters: Lucy and Ellen, but we tried to ignore them. I had not yet discovered girls.

John and I were about the same age, so most of my time was with him. We were big on playing "Tarzan." I recall the numerous grape vines in the trees near their home. It was a perfect setting for a couple of boys with sharpened wooden spears who thought they were in the jungle. But, unlike the many "Tarzan" films, those old grapevines occasionally broke. It was similar to "Murphy's Law" the higher up you were, the more likely the vine would give way.

John's father, I remember, had been a bombardier during World War II. I can still recall photographs hanging on their living room walls depicting those old planes as they dropped tons of bombs on the Germans. Those pictures always fascinated me. Of course, at age 10 or 11, excitement, intrigue, and fascination were only a grapevine away.

Although the Morris Family had "stepped up" in the world by the move to Lake Creek, we were still poor by the world's standards. Even the poor people called us poor. And by the word "poor," I am speaking in regard to money. We were just the same as our neighbors – without funds. We had everything else.

There were several migrant families around the community. They were usually there for a year or two, then they were gone, following seasonal crop harvests.

I remember my brother and I had talked Dad into getting some white rabbits. We built cages for them, watching them grow into full grown pets. But like most boys, we were not all that responsible. One day, after feeding the rabbits, one of us (I will always think it was David. Why would I leave the door ajar?) left the cage door open. The next morning, they were all gone. We searched everywhere, but no white rabbits.

A few days later, one of the migrant workers spoke to my Father. During their conversation, the man said, "I didn't know there were white rabbits in this part of the country. They sure cooked up good."

No more rabbits for the Morris boys.

David and I loved to shoot. Our Father taught us gun safety

and the art of firing a long gun (rifle or shotgun) from the time we were old enough to understand. You might say, "We cut our teeth on a Remington, single-shot, .22-Caliber Rifle." We were also proficient with a shotgun.

Dad was the best shot I have ever known. Roy Rogers, Gene Autry, John Wayne, Tex Ritter, Lash Larue, Bob Steel, nor the Lone Ranger could come close to his marksmanship. We regularly watched as he threw up pennies and shot them away with his old Remington .22 rifle. I can remember a few misses, but not many. He rarely missed anything he shot at. Sometimes (I think it was just to "show-off") he would take his rifle when we were going quail hunting. More often than not, he would come home with more quail than either of us. You guessed it; he shot them on the fly with a .22 caliber rifle. That was some shooting! I have also seen him shoot flies off an old fence around our yard or strike matches stuck in the fence. You could see the fly one minute and then a small bullet hole where the fly had been. I'll always remember his marksmanship and his quiet demeanor. I don't ever recall him bragging about anything, other than his boys.

Years later, David and I would become two of the first Police Combat Firearms Instructors with the Oklahoma Department of Corrections. I like to think that our Father taught us the basics needed to accomplish that envied status. I still miss him today, but especially, when I pick up a firearm.

But enough of that; I'm still a kid living at Lake Creek.

One of my dearest and most cherished childhood memories has to be the ice cream suppers and the all-night Forty-Two games. The adults took care of the domino games while the kids took care of the ice cream. It was a fair trade-off.

Jim Hays was the owner and long time operator of the Hays Welding Shop in Willow, a small town about six miles from our home.

Jim was a man with a gift for building and repairing things. He could make false teeth, sharpen a plow, repair your watch or make

29

a suit of clothes. In addition to his talents relating to metal, he was somewhat of a philosopher. He was also one of my Father's best friends.

Jim and his family regularly came to our house, always bringing his movie projector. I recall hanging bed sheets between two trees then sitting back to watch a Roy Rogers or Gene Autry movie. Sometimes, Jim had a John Wayne, Tex Ritter, or Lash Larue Movie. The ones I remember best had Gabby Hays in them; he was one of my favorite characters.

I don't think I have mentioned it, but I actually met Gabby a few years later during the time when I was (required) to attend high school. Like many young people of that time, I had a job away from the farm. I was working for Clarence Snow at the Willow Service Station. I was slaving away one day when a white Cadillac convertible slid to a stop in the gravel driveway. I recognized the man instantly because of his twisted smirk, crumpled Stetson and white beard. He looked at me, standing in the station doorway, and said, "Young man, how in the hell does a person get out of this country?" I enjoyed giving him directions back to Interstate 40, some 30 miles away. I don't recall whether he thanked me, but he did appear to be in somewhat of a hurry as he floored the Cadillac, throwing gravel everywhere. Perhaps he had a film to shoot.

That was the first time I had met someone who was famous, not to mention, one of my favorite actors. I was impressed, even after sweeping the gravel out of the station.

THE WILLOW SERVICE STATION

It was bound to happen. My hormones had kicked in and I had stumbled onto the opposite sex. I had discovered girls!

Along with this startling discovery and life altering revelation, things began to change at Lake Creek. School attendance dropped, people started moving out of the country into local towns and we were faced with the dreaded word, consolidation. I don't think I knew what the word meant at the time, but I quickly learned that we were losing our school; we were going to Granite. How embarrassing. We didn't need those "town people" telling us how to act. What had we done to deserve such a travesty or miscarriage of the learning process? Was it the sandburs in the teacher's chair or the mouse in her desk? We would fight this to the end.

But we had lost, and in 1957, the unthinkable happened; we started to school at Granite.

But wait, this wasn't so bad. There were lots of pretty girls gathering together, blinking their eyes at us "new kids." Things could work out after all.

That was when I discovered Linda Marie Brooks. Wow! Before you could say, "Her dad is mean as hell," I was visiting Ms Linda almost every day. After all, I had a Cushman Motor Scooter and it was only 13 miles to Granite from our farm. I would learn about her three younger brothers and father later. But now, I must return to the Willow Service Station.

I was 14 or 15 when I began working at the Willow Service Station. Clarence Snow, the operator, quickly became my mentor, best friend and, of course, my boss. Clarence was around 50 years old at the time, well versed in almost every subject, but especially, women. As that was a relatively foreign subject to someone like me, I took in everything he had to say. Looking back, I now realize some of his advise was good and some not so good. I guess no one can be perfect all the time.

Clarence was not the only advisor I faced; the station was a "hangout" for local farmers and everyone else with time on their hands. It was a good place to catch up on all the latest news; who was doing what or who was seeing who, etc. Some people would call that gossip, but that was for the women. Men exchange news, I was told.

Owen Campbell (better known to all of us as "Eightball") quickly became another of my friends. Eightball came to the Willow area after the War. He had no family and was immediately adopted by the whole community. He was somewhat of a character but was a friend and helper to everyone. What I remember most about him was his dry sense of humor and the little known fact that he never wore underwear. The underwear thing certainly was not an issue with me. I could easily understand why a man objected to another piece of clothing to wash. I thought it was a great idea, but one my Mother did not agree with.

One day, Eightball and Clarence decided to have a race. They were always joking with each other about how much faster their pickup was compared to the other.

I was to be with Eightball and my brother with Clarence. The rules were simple. We would both leave the station, drive one mile in opposite directions, then meet back at the station. The first one back was the winner and the loser would be required to "buy the cokes." (This phrase was used several times each day at the station)

Time for the race. Both trucks left at about the same time in a cloud of dust. When all the dust cleared, Eightball and I were sitting in his pickup behind the station. A few minutes later, Clarence and David drove up finding us in the station drinking our free coke. The only thing Eightball said was, "You lost, Snowball." Nothing was ever said about us never leaving the station. I guess they just bought it "hook, line and sinker," or did they?

There were other "colorful" characters in and out of the station every day. Lynn Mayfield always brought a few laughs, and sometimes "gasps" to the generally mundane crew at Clarence's Station.

Lynn was in his late 60s or early 70s, lived alone and was known for his strange lifestyle – that is putting it mildly. He always carried a pistol, or so I was told. It was rumored that he had killed a man at some point in his life, but no one was able to come up with the exact circumstance or time. It was just one of those stories that grew with each passing year. I suspect that by the time I was 20 years old, Lynn would have been responsible for the brutal murders of entire families, probably, with a double-bit ax or chainsaw, on Good Friday.

Lynn drove everywhere, but at about 40 mph. It was not unusual to find him driving along in another state with 20 vehicles stacked up behind him, occasionally blowing their horns. He would never alter his speed. For those of us who knew him, 40 mph was just fine. No one crossed Lynn or cautioned him regarding his driving or any of his bizarre activities.

I suppose you could say Lynn had developed some less than normal eating habits. It was just a normal occurrence to watch him pluck a nice, green grasshopper from the side of one of the two gas pumps, then pop it in his mouth as if it were just another bite of Sunday dinner. It initially almost made me sick at my stomach, but I got used to it. The only thing that really bothered me was when one of those grasshoppers tried to escape and its legs would protrude out of Lynn's mouth. That really grossed me out, but I never said anything.

Frankie Vitosky was always good for a few laughs. He was a local farmer, always in a hurry. Much like Gabby Hayes' arrival, Frankie would come sliding into the driveway, almost running into the station or gas pumps. He usually needed a quart of oil and "filler up with regular."

I could never get the hood to lock down, while Frankie would be standing there fidgeting nervously. He would normally take over and close the hood.

One day, he could not get the hood latch to cooperate. He climbed up on top of the car, jumping off as he planted both feet squarely on the hood. He locked it, believe me, but it was now about two inches below the fenders. Frankie would jump in his old car, and like Gabby Hayes, threw gravel all over the place.

Frankie is still in a hurry today.

Calvin Vanzandt, (my cousin) and I were constantly together as we neared 16 years of age. He was at my house much of the time or I was a regular in his home.

One day I was working at the station when a beer truck rounded the corner on its way to Willow. The driver must have been in a hurry because he appeared to have made the curve on two wheels. As he turned, one of the doors came open and several cases of beer fell to the pavement. Since there was no one around and he didn't know he had lost part of his load, I quickly gathered the spoils and hid them. It was like Christmas, only earlier.

When I got off work, Calvin and I made a valiant attempt at disposing of all that beer. We also had a gallon of wine and had little difficulty in working it into our drink-fest. We barely made it to my house. I remember my Dad caught on fairly quick, but my Mother couldn't put it all together. Every time we took a drink of water, we were sick again. I think my Father knew this would be a self-correcting problem, because he didn't have much to say. He simply smiled when one of us made a dash for the bathroom or backyard. I have never been so sick.

HAYSTACK

In north central Greer County, in an area known as the "Breaks," stands a landmark known as Haystack Mountain. It is an unusual formation because it is shaped like a hay stack. It shares the unusual area with a small creek known as Haystack Creek, which is occasionally out of banks during the rainy season - when there is a rainy season.

The "Breaks" is an area of gypsum rock and red clay soil that has eroded over the years until it appears more like the moon's surface than the United States.

Haystack is capped off at the top with a section of white gypsum rock which makes the formation stand out for miles.

When I was a teenager, there wasn't much I didn't get into. On this particular day, and being at my best - for a teenager - I was with some friends at Haystack. We had decided to climb up the side, sit a while at the top, then try to dislodge some larger rocks then watch them roll to the bottom. If that sounds boring to you, think about being 15 or 16 again with not much to do. That's better.

To the top we go. It didn't take long to reach the top, after all, we were in our teens. At the top, we followed our original plan; we sat a while, smoked cigarettes (anything forbidden), talked about girls and whatever boys talk about. After things began to slow down, we decided to try our hands at rolling rocks off the top. One of my friends had an old rail-job (a vehicle with only the frame, engine and place to sit) he had parked on the east side of Haystack.

With keen observation and clear heads, we decided to dislodge a huge gypsum rock on the west side, thereby sparing the rail-job any further damage - simply being a rail-job was damage enough.

It took some sweat and time, but four of us finally managed to free a boulder about the size of a small living room couch - and the same shape. We didn't know how it would roll, but were more than happy to give it a test run. Our plan was simply - much like our minds - we would start the rock off the west side by shoving with all our might, then, sit down and watch what happened. How's that for simplicity. Who said teenagers were complicated.

We got a good roll. We stared in blank silence as the huge rock began to roll end over end in a tight, right-hand pattern. Soon it was going down the northwest side, then the north, then the northeast side, then the east side.

"There's no way it's going to hit the rail-job. It would be such an unlucky thing to happen. There's just no way." These were our words of encouragement to ourselves and to the owner of the "used-to-be" vehicle. "The way the rock is turning, it will miss the car by a mile."

With many other words of encouragement, we continued to bolster the spirits of our friend. With odds and slim chances, we had convinced him the car was completely safe.

But, can you guess what happened? I thought so. Yes it was more or less a direct hit, a broadside, diatribe, onslaught, barrage, volley, strike, an attack. It was as if God had willed it to happen. Or, perhaps aliens had flown over Haystack and turned everything around. They were known to do such things in that part of the country. It was probably just an act of God.

I have never seen that much dust before, but then, I had never seen a car hit by a rock the size of a divan. It was almost total destruction. We continued to stand in awe. It was just awful.

After going down to survey the total obliteration of the "rail-job," we felt certain the steering wheel could be salvaged - maybe.

QUICK DRAW AND STUPIDITY

Looking back at some of the things I did as a young man, it's a miracle I'm still around. I know my parents would turn over in their graves if they knew some of the things my brother and I did.

As I said before, we were both excellent shots with rifles. In fact, we have been guilty of determining just how close we could shoot to each other without drawing blood. I think both of us had some jeans with bullet holes in the pants legs. Now, that's the height of stupidity.

But perhaps the stunts my cousin, Jerry Don Henderson, and I managed to survive, they were probably even worse. I don't recall why our parents allowed us to possess .22-caliber pistols, but they did. It has crossed my mind that they secretly hoped we would shoot each other. That's what we did.

We both had the low-slung holsters like Roy Rogers and Gene Autry, without, of course, brains. I'm not sure teenagers have fully functional brains until they are out of their teens.

We were good. In fact, we struggled with a way to test our quick-draw ability against each other. Who was the fastest? We finally devised a plan that would for certain, determine, once and for all, who was the king of fast-draw. It was ingenious, but stupid.

We carefully removed the lead from our bullets, careful not to loose any powder, then replaced the lead with wet cloth. It was a wonderful idea, at the time. Of course, the brilliance of a teenage boy is similar to a bolt of lightening; here one moment and gone the next. In fact, I don't believe you should use those words (brilliance and teenage boy) in the same sentence.

Anyway, the contest was on. We stood across the bed from each other, taking turns counting to three. Oh, did I mention we had removed our shirts? I thought not. On the count of three, we would draw and fire.

I don't know why, but we thought those bits of cloth wouldn't hurt when they hit our bare skin - wrong. They hurt like hell, in fact, I don't know that we shouldn't have left the lead in our shells.

We never determined who was the king of quick-draw. We were both ready to quit after the first few whelps on our chests. We were fortunate we weren't killed. I think I may still have some of those tiny scars.

Can you believe I would grow up to be a Oklahoma State Certified Police Combat Firearms Instructor with The Counsel on Law Enforcement Training and Education? Amazing, simply amazing.

HORSES AND ROPES

As a teenager, I was on a horse much of the time. I had friends who rode, and usually on the weekends, three or four of us were riding off in some direction. Danny Martin and the Bagwell Boys (James and Jerry) were my good friends and riding buddies. We often ventured north of the river to an area known as Horseshoe Bluffs or Horseshoe Mountain, although it was neither. It was a clay and gypsum formation, much like Haystack, that had eroded over the years causing it to take on the appearance of a horseshoe. The sides were very steep, not allowing us to ride to the top, however, at the back, it opened up with a gradual slope. From that area, we were able to ride all the way to the top. We carved our names on gypsum rock at the top each time we visited.

I fancied myself a good roper in those days. My Father had spent hours and hours teaching me how to use the lariat. I wasn't bad with a loop. I always carried a rope on my saddle when we were riding. Sometimes, it was necessary to pull a fence post over to gain passage to our desired riding destination, but we always put them back.

One day, we were riding a couple of miles from our house, along the road near Harley Locklear's place. Harley's house was about a quarter-mile off the main road, but was clearly visible from the backs of our mounts. Harley also had a beautiful welded-chain mailbox. It had a nice curve in the large, linked chain that was welded to an old truck rim. It was nice and shiny with a fresh coat of silver paint making it irresistible to a young, mischievous rider with a rope. As we rode by, I dropped a loop over the mailbox and pulled it over.

As I was off my horse retrieving the rope, we heard Harley's pickup come to life. We could see him coming as fast as the old truck would run.

And run is what we did. We took off down the road searching for a place to go. As there were fences on both sides of the road, we had to ride several hundred yards before we were able to get out of the road into a field. We rode out in a field, stopping about 200 yards from the road. Harley slid to a stop and jumped out of the old pickup. He was obviously angry as he stomped around with both hands on his hips shouting, "Who are you?" We knew he couldn't see well enough to identify us. I stood up in my stirrups, cupped my hands while shouting back at him, "I don't know." This went on for a few minutes before he left. I don't think Harley ever knew who we were.

Although his mailbox was not hurt, I always regretted pulling it over, especially with him watching.

GIRLS

As I neared 16, I bought my first car. I traded the Cushman in on a 1954 Chevrolet. It was light green and white, a straight six-cylinder and the prettiest thing I had ever seen – with the exception of Linda Marie Brooks.

Things were beginning to come together. I had a car, and a girl. What more could a person want? I was in for a rude awakening.

I began to spend much more time in Granite at the Brooks house. But her Father (Chig) had other plans. He always made certain he answered the door when I showed up. He would jerk the door open and say, "What the hell are you doing here?" He also encouraged the boys, Doc, Guy and Bill, to do their part in "running the sand flea back to the country."

One day after leaving Linda's house, I discovered the boys had stolen my car. They had pushed it down the alley as far as they could, which really made me mad. I chased Doc, who was the oldest, across the street then through a barbed wire fence. I did catch him, but discovered I could not kill him - too many witnesses. I also tore my new slacks on the barbed wire. It was not a good day.

On another occasion, I was greeted at the Brooks house with a barrage of ripe tomatoes. Linda's brothers had climbed up on the basketball goal with a large bucket of tomatoes. As soon as I stepped out of my car, they drew first blood- so to speak. Maintaining a relationship with Linda was difficult. Chig and the boys were always up to something, but I had made up my mind they would not discourage this "sand flea".

1958

I had made it to 16, though no fault of my own. My brother had been out of school for a couple of years, had joined the United States Air Force; I actually missed him .

Things were going well on the farm. Dad had dug the first irrigation well in that part of the country and it was a real gusher. I remember Fount Huggins, the driller, pulled almost completely round rocks out of the drill shaft, then made the comment that there was an "underground river down there." He said it was one of the best irrigation wells he had ever drilled.

We were now able to water cotton and peanuts. Those first few years were really profitable ones. I can't say much about the hand-move irrigation system, but that was the only thing available back then and we were happy to have it.

By hand-move, I mean a person had to move each 30' section of pipe by hand. We did that twice each day – usually a quarter-mile. The operation consisted of taking off, or adding, two 30' mainline sections of pipe which made the move 60'. Watering 24 hours each day, we were able to cross a field fairly quickly, but it was hard work. Carrying a 30' section of irrigation pipe (with a sprinkler riser on the end) took some practice to obtain the proper balance. After a few hundred, it became easy to pick one up at the correct spot for balance.

I was at that age when fast cars were constantly on my mind. I made several mistakes in that area, but the most glowing plunder was when I traded a perfectly good automobile for a late model Chevrolet Impala. It was fast. With three, two-barreled carburetors and a positive traction rear end, it would pass everything but a service station.

I recall bringing it home for the first time. My Dad walked

around it a couple of times, kicked the tires and shook his head, then made the comment I will always remember, "Well, it seems to have a good steering wheel." He was correct in his assessment. My latest trade had 2 cracked pistons, requiring major work. Lesson learned the hard way.

1960

At 18, and like most young men of that age, I thought I knew everything. Looking back at those times, I am amazed at my absolute stupidity. But I was graduating from high school with hopes of attending college. Linda and I were still together, and things had eased up somewhat with her father and the boys. We were all hunting together, I was playing guitar in a band with Linda's uncle, Thurman Brooks and my relationship with Chig was better. I was also attending their family reunion each year playing the guitar with family members. Linda and I were talking about marriage, but that had to wait two years until she was out of high school.

David and his wife, Linda, were back on the farm after he was discharged from the Air Force.

1962

Probably the happiest day of my life, Linda and I were married June 16, 1962, at the Baptist Church in Granite. It was a beautiful wedding with her father giving her away as scheduled. We had some doubt about that happening, but Linda's uncle, Thurman, said he would give the bride away if Chig refused. It was a sad day for him, but he managed to follow through, even through the tears. I recall feeling sorry for him.

We had an 8'x36' mobile home set up in Sayre, Oklahoma where I was to attend college. We didn't realize how small and cramped our new home was, and we didn't care. Our new married life was the important thing.

Then everything came crashing down. My Father suffered a cerebral hemorrhage. He would spend the next several months in St. Anthony's Hospital in Oklahoma City. I suppose he was fortunate to survive, but he would never be the same. It was devastating for all of us. He was our hero, our best friend, our teacher and guide through the life we had just started. I remember thinking it was like losing myself. How could we go on without our guide?

But like anything in this life, we learned to live with the hand we were dealt. Dad slowly began to regain some of his memory and motor skills and before long was doing some less strenuous chores around the farm. Although things were not the same, he was still with us.

Linda and I moved back to the farm where we began working the land. My brother and I would continue to farm for the next few years in order to pay off loans against our farms. We raised cattle, farmed and irrigated cotton and peanuts. Both our wives worked off the farm as cosmetologists, after completing that training. Our Mother remained on the farm caring for Father. Those were some difficult years for all of us, but they would get worse.

In 1967, our first daughter was born - Shannon Jill Morris. She was the most beautiful baby I had ever seen. I remember sitting down in the floor at the Mangum Hospital and crying. I don't know why, perhaps just sheer joy.

Things were beginning to become more difficult on the farm. My brother had two sons and the Morris Family had become nine people living off what should have been a one-person operation.

David was the first to seek work off the farm. He was hired at the Oklahoma State Reformatory, Oklahoma Department of Corrections as a Security Officer. I began driving a school bus for the Granite School system, which meant we were all working, but getting nowhere. Something had to change.

In 1968, I became a full time Security Officer for the Oklahoma Department of Corrections. There were approximately 700 inmates at the prison in Granite and security was much different than today. We had an open yard as well as dormitories, but things seemed to work well because we were allowed to enforce the rules.

I remember my first day on the job. My father-in-law, Chig Brooks, also worked at the prison and was the person who introduced me to the "inside." He first took me into the open yard where I met some of the employees and inmates. One particular guard was "Skoot" Nickell. He was a huge man with a temper to match his size. Everyone knew he carried a pair of brass knucks in his pocket, ready to use them without hesitation.

Skoot was sitting under the domino shed on the "black" side of the yard (that was still in the days of segregation). He called a young black man over, telling him, "Hey, Bulldog, cuss for this new man." I will never forget some of the language I heard that day. I felt as though I had lived under a rock most of my life or at the bottom of a well. I listened to words I had never thought of, much less, heard. I began to have second thoughts about my new vocation. When "Bulldog" had finished with his "cussing for the new man" he was told to go back and sit down. The scene was reminiscent of someone telling their dog to "go lay down and shut up." It was a real eye-opener for me.

As with any new job, a person usually begins with the work no one else wants. My first assignment was at the South Dormitory. I would supervise 60 blacks on the west side and 60 whites on the east end of the building, with my office located in the center. I had nothing to protect myself with, as security personnel on the inside were not allowed to have any type of weapon.

I did have a few inmates who would help me break up a fight, but primarily, an officer in the south dormitory was alone. The main rotunda was several hundred yards away. When help was needed, it took at least 15 minutes for other officers to show up, not to mention the fact that we were usually short-handed.

My first Sergeant was Mr. Blackburn. He was a huge man with a very dry sense of humor and exemplary work ethics. He was very strict but a man with great compassion. He was one of the finest men I have ever known. The only thing I had against him was the fact that he teamed me with Sam Davis when I worked the west cell house.

Sam was a good man, but hated the blacks and they felt the same way about him. For that reason, Sam worked the top two runs where the whites were housed, along with "light" solitary confinement, and I worked "lockup" and dark solitary confinement, along with the bottom two runs where blacks were housed. At night when things were quiet and boring, Sam would come down stairs and invariable, start an argument with some of the men on my runs. When they began to be loud, he would simply go back upstairs. As I said, Sam was a good man and a good officer, but he was full of practical jokes and pranks. He did, however, help me out several times when things got a little crazy.

One night, I had an inmate escape from his cell after forcing paper into the door locking mechanism. Prisoners often did that when a complete section of doors was locked. That particular door would fail to lock, but without interfering with other doors. It was sometimes difficult to detect until an officer found an inmate in the wrong cell or simply out running around. That was the case with the inmate that night. The only difference was that he was drunk on home brew. The man was an Indian, twice my size. I was attempting to "herd" him back toward his cell with very little luck. The real problem arose when he came up with a mop handle and decided he didn't want to go "home." The man had me cornered at the back of the cell house, but was beginning to listen to me when Sam sneaked up behind the guy and put him to sleep with a pick handle. There were other instances involving Sam, but most I can't mention.

Homemade weapons were an ongoing problem inside the walls; I'm sure nothing has changed today. The weapons were made from everything imaginable; old steel springs, tooth brushes, steak or pork chop bones, wooden shingles, steel rods of all kinds, spoons, combs and just about anything imaginable. When it comes to protecting themselves, prison inmates are extremely resourceful.

Sam and I had just "racked" the doors on "light sol" in order to take the prisoners out for a shower. One of the offenders stepped out of his cell with a flattened spoon, sharpened all around, and began cutting on another inmate. Blood was everywhere, even on the ceiling. I shouted at the man to drop the weapon, which he did, but by the time Sam and I got to the injured man, he had lost a great deal of blood. We were able to save his life, but it was a close call for him.

Incidents such as that were common at OSR. There was never a dull moment. When things seemed to be going well, you knew something was coming. It could be fires, fights, attempted escapes, anything you could imagine.

Usually, inmates set their cells on fire in protest of something. We had an inmate who was locked up in holding for some type of disciplinary action. He was always protesting something. I think this time, he was unhappy with the food he was receiving.

I was sitting at the end of the lockup area at around midnight when I detected smoke. I was up walking the runs when I located the source of fire to be on lockup. An inmate on holding had set fire to his mattress, bedding and was standing at his door waiting for someone to open it.

I went back to my post and sat down. He began to scream and I could see flames, periodically, come through the open bars on the door. When I finally opened his door, he jumped out onto the run with his clothing on fire. Once they were extinguished, we made him clean up his cell, refusing to give him more bedding or a mattress. For the next several nights, he slept on a steel frame with nothing else. To my knowledge, he never set another fire.

David and I were working full time off the farm and working our land on weekends. This would go on for several more years.

After nine months in security, I changed jobs and became a Classification Officer with the prison. This was more of a counseling position and working with inmates on a variety of problems and issues.

After a short time, I began working for Vocational Rehabilitative Services at the Reformatory, testing inmates for a psychologist and performing clerk duties for four Vocational Specialists.

I remember Jack Plummer, the psychologist very well. Jack

was a severe diabetic who would not take care of himself. We would often find him wandering around the institution unable to tell you who he was or why he was there. We normally kept candy to revive him.

Jack was a strange sort of character, who enjoyed barbeque goat, often inviting us to one of his parties. I always managed to get out of going with some lame excuse. I didn't care for goat.

Jack was a good psychologist, but was always conducting some strange experiment. He once set up a series of mirrors at the prison's hog barn to monitor their reactions at seeing themselves. I never knew hogs were particularly interested in how they looked, or they would stay out of the mud, but that was just my opinion. Anyway, Jack burned the hog barn to the ground with his mirrors. Apparently the sun hit one of mirrors at just the right angle, and started a fire. All the hogs were lost, along with his experiment.

I was sitting in my office one day when Calvin Vincent came in and sat down. Calvin was the District V Supervisor for Probation and Parole out of the Arnett, Oklahoma office. He asked if I would be interested in a position as Institutional Parole Officer. I was interested and took the job.

For the next couple of years, I worked as Institutional Parole Officer. There were only two of us in the state - Granite and at McAlester. We screened inmates for parole, worked up all the necessary paper work, and supplied the information to the Pardon and Parole Board.

1973

The year of 1973 would prove to be my most difficult year. My Father died. I could never truly prepare for his death, although I knew the day would come. Again, we were all devastated, but life would go on.

A bright spot in our lives came that year when we adopted our second daughter, Sharra. She was two months old when we drove to Oklahoma City and picked her up. From that time on, she would be my buddy. Both my girls were very special to me, as they are today. In 1973, I also left the Reformatory and began working as a field officer with Probation and Parole. The Institutional Parole Officer Position was abolished as the work was delegated to Correctional Personnel. I was ready to begin work as a field officer, or so I thought.

I inherited a caseload of approximately 100 people spread out over six counties in Western Oklahoma: Harmon, Greer, Beckham, Custer, Roger Mills and Ellis. I also did some work in the panhandle, at times. The area was the complete second judicial district which had not been worked in over six months. The former officer had died after suffering a heart attack several months before. It would prove to be a nightmare, especially with as little training as I had.

James Morgan was a Probation and Parole Officer in the Newkirk area and the District sent him to Western Oklahoma to train me. Jim was a former police officer with great insight when it came to understanding people. His low-key approach, friendly demeanor and his on-going humor were only a few of his many good qualities that made him one of the best officers in the state. I will never forget one of his many "sayings." I think this was his favorite: "If you can't dazzle them with brilliance, baffle them with bull shit."

Jim and I spent two days meeting judges and law enforcement in my area. We also met a few of the people on my caseload – the few we could find. I remember fording the river near Hollis, in search of a client. You would have to understand the Harmon County area to understand the general lay-of-the-land.

After two days, we loaded a hundred or so case files into the trunk of my state vehicle along with a couple of boxes of assorted forms. Jim drove off as he told me, "I'll see you at the district meeting in Arnett next month. Keep your head down."

I was completely lost. I searched for people for days, closed cases, wrote violation reports and established contact with officials in my area. At night, I would spread out client files in the living room floor, taking inventory, writing field contact notes, while making other notations. Linda filed reports, maintained some order in my cases, and typed court documents. I could not have made it without her.

RABIES

My brother and I would continue to farm for several years in addition to working at our other jobs with the Department of Corrections.

Few things on the farm strike more fear in the heart, than the word, "Rabies." This infectious disease is a viral infection of certain warm-blooded animals, caused by a virus in the Rhabdovridae family. Once it is active and attacks the nervous system, it is 100 percent fatal, if not treated.

In our section of the United States, the disease occurs mainly in skunks, raccoons, fox, and bats, however, can appear in small rodents such as beavers, chipmunks, squirrels, rats, and mice.

The incubation in humans from the time of exposure to the onset of illness can vary, but usually ranges anywhere from five days to a year. Symptoms may also vary, but often includes vomiting, itching or numbness, tingling, and pain. The virus enters the body through a cut or scratch, or through mucous membranes, then travels to the central nervous system. Once it reaches the brain, it travels to different organs and multiplies. At that point, it is normally fatal.

We usually ran anywhere from 100 to 200 head of cattle, primarily, a cow-calf operation. Although not unusual to lose a few head of cattle every year, the loss of three seemingly healthy calves drew our attention.

The first young, bull calf was found dead with no apparent wounds anywhere on its skin. We probed the animal, opened its mouth, etc., in an effort to determine the cause of death. The next two calves were treated the same when it was determined no wounds were visible. We finally took one of the dead animals to

Dr. Charles Freeman, a Veterinarian in Hobart, Oklahoma.
I recall Dr. Freeman calling that particular morning. He informed me that we would all be required to take the rabies vaccine. Cold chills consumed my entire body because of the horror stories I had heard about the "shots." But, regardless of the pain, it had to be done. I also regretted having to inform two of my neighbors who stopped and helped us load the animals in a stock trailer.

Our next step was to contact the State Health Department informing them of the incident and beginning our inoculations. We would be taking the older vaccine which was made from duck embryo and very painful, we were told. It would be a series of 14 shots which would be in the fatty part of the stomach. If an individual missed a day, it would require that the process start all over again.

David and I took our inoculations at the same time. The first one was no worse than a simple flu shot, causing me some feeling of relief. But the next day, the second shot was more like a red-hot metal rod being jammed into my stomach; it hurt like hell. It was not only the pain, but the red, hard knots in my stomach after each shot that made me sick at my stomach.

From the first shot to the last, I was sick. I had knots under my arms, in my neck, but the worst were the 14, hard, red knots in my stomach. Occasionally, the nurse would hit the edge of one of those knots as she gave me the shot. I think that was probably the most painful.

I have always told my brother that the shots helped him. They didn't seem to cause any problems for him, or any of the other men.

By the end of the ordeal, I had decided that the cure was as bad as rabies.

That nightmare would cause me to declare war on skunks. From that day on, I would kill everyone I ran across, whether in the road, ditch, or running out across a field, if within range. I have even run off the road (not far) to run them down. I learned, if you hit them with one of the front tires, they rarely smell - sometimes.

THEY STILL HANG CATTLE THIEVES,
DON'T THEY?

If you're thinking I didn't get the training I needed, you are correct. In those days, we learned from the "School of Hard Knocks" and by trial and error. Most of our training was one-on-one with another officer as Jim Morgan had done with me. We simply didn't have enough time to go through much training, so we relied upon other officers for what we needed to know. I did spend a few days with my supervisor, again, on the road trying to locate offenders.

I had a case on an old gentleman who lived on a small ranch just across the Packsaddle Bridge in Ellis County. I would estimate his age, at the time, at 75, although he was still very active and was in good health. He was on parole for Larceny of Domestic Animals (cattle) but it was not his first offense. As I remember, he had served numerous terms for the same offense.

As Calvin and I drove into the man's property, we noted the cattle pen was holding several head of cattle. With no bill of sale, it did not take long to determine they were stolen. Several different brands on the animals would later be traced back to ranchers in the general area. My supervisor, who also farmed and ranched on the side, was not happy with the situation.

As I talked with the old man, we both watched as my boss walked to the car, opened the truck and removed a lariat. He began to fashion a hangman's noose in one end as he started walking around under the large cottonwood trees. He was whistling as he twirled the rope while searching for a low-hanging limb.

The old man looked at me and asked, "He's not serious, is he?" I didn't really know if he was serious, but quickly answered, "You know him better than I do, you tell me." The old man's facial color changed to a chalky white. He was not really disappointed when we took him to jail. Some people never learn.

THE 1973 MCALESTER RIOT

I was just beginning to settle into my work when the Oklahoma State Penitentiary was almost destroyed in the worst prison riot in the history of our country.

Prison officials knew of on-going problems, but had little information concerning what would take place. It all started when a few inmates with knives began encouraging other inmates to join them. As their numbers picked up, they went into the mess hall where they stabbed two officers. Then, the inmates began to take hostages. Before long, they took over the public address system and announced, "We have taken over. We have weapons and hostages. It's a revolution - come and help us."

Within only a few minutes, OSP was into a full-scale riot. They took over the hospital area where they began taking various drugs, then they were in the paint shop where many inmates started sniffing paint and other chemicals. Soon, buildings were set ablaze with the number of hostages rising to 14. All buildings on the south side of the compound were now burning. Inmates had run of the yard and other areas, as the number of hostages rose to around 20. Utilities were out, with the only lights visible coming from the numerous buildings now engulfed in flames.

Before the riot ended, four inmates were dead and the damage to the state's largest prison was estimated to be from 20 to 40 million dollars.

Probation and Parole Officers were sent in shifts to assist Correctional Officers and Law Enforcement Officers deal with the McAlester riot.

I remember - very vividly - lining up with other officers at the front tower before entering the facility. The fires were still burning and the screams and yelling from inside the walls made the hair stand up on the back of my neck. Although armed, it was a scary place to be walking into. We were to search for inmates who could be hiding and provide security inside the walls.

Just as we were going up the front steps, the officer on the front tower accidentally discharged a Thompson Machine Gun into the air. I have never been one to fear much of anything, but I don't mind saying; I was scared!

I knew the first inmate I saw as I entered the rotunda. His head bore the imprint of chain links as he asked if I knew who his case manager was. I ordered him to sit down inside the rotunda area. We rotated in shifts at OSP for several months. I remember my hands turning green from the number of handcuffs and leg irons put on or removed from inmates. I was glad when the assignment was over.

There were many reasons for the riot; overcrowding, refusal of Governor Hall to sign parole recommendations, low correctional officer pay ($380.00 mo.) inmate abuse, continued racial segregation, censorship, poor health care, poor food and idleness. The State of Oklahoma would find itself under years of federal court order. It would be an expensive lesson.

HUNGRY SNIPERS

There were often disturbances at the Oklahoma State Reformatory, however, most of them were minor. When they were serious, with lives at risk, my brother and I were sometimes called to act as snipers. This was prior to the Department of Corrections having Tactical Personnel, or specialized teams.

I was notified one morning of a serious riot at the prison and asked to go to one of the back towers in order to cover the kitchen area. Inmates had taken hostages in the kitchen area, had barricaded the entries, but no one had been injured.

I picked up a scoped rifle and was on the tower within a few minutes. I think my brother was on top of the administration building watching the northern yard and the front of the kitchen.

My view of the kitchen was primarily the south entry and an inmate who was acting as sentry. I was lying on the concrete run watching through a scope, praying for the hostages, while hoping I would not be forced to shoot anyone. I maintained that position for several hours before the inmate at the side door, finally saw me on the run. From that time on, all I saw was the piece of a mirror and the inmates eye reflection.

The inmates inside the kitchen had made certain demands to prison administrators and were cooking and eating steaks. I could occasionally pick up the smell of food coming from the facility. The Correctional Officer and I on the tower were about to starve. We had nothing to eat since the day before. Things were not looking so good for us on this day, either. At least we had water.

Although I was younger at that time, I can assure you that lying on a concrete run looking through a scope for hours, is not easy. But my primary concerns were the hostages inside the kitchen.

Someone finally came by and tossed a couple of apples up to us. That was the best piece of fruit I had ever eaten.

The situation was finally resolved when the administration and inmate leaders came to some agreement. No one was injured.

LIFE IN THE FIELD

I will have to admit, I had led a sheltered life up that point. I had spent most of my life on the farm having never been exposed to some of the more nauseating circumstances in the world. I was about to get a quick and enlightening education.

I remember one of the first people I contacted, was a young black man in Hollis. I had gone to his home to make contact, but quickly noticed that the front door of the home was missing. I was about to leave, thinking the house was vacant, when I saw a man walk out into the yard.

There had been a light snow the night before, as the seasons were in the process of changing. After getting out of my car and visiting with the young man, I asked about the missing door. He said he simply could not afford to buy one. Upon closer examination, I could see that snow had drifted into his bedroom and had accumulated under his bed. I couldn't believe anyone could live in circumstances like that. I felt ashamed that I had so much and this man had so little.

I can't recall the reason this man was under state supervision, but I remember thinking at the time, no one deserves this standard of living, regardless of his crime – not in the land of plenty.

The next thing I did made a life-long impression on this young man. We got in my vehicle, went to town where I purchased a door for his house. We then returned and I helped him install it.

As I said, I can't remember the man's name, but I know he still remembers mine, although that has been about 40 years ago.

To this day, I can still see that young man's face and the gratitude in his eyes. This was the sort of work I wanted to do, I thought.

THE BLUE-FRONT BAR

Harmon County was one of the poorest areas I worked as an officer. Located in extreme Southwest Oklahoma, it bordered Texas, and at times, experienced a high crime rate for a county its size.

Although it was a successful farming community, many of the farm workers drawn to the county were Hispanic and African American without roots or family ties in the area.

I remember one of my co-workers at the time, referred to Harmon County as the "Arm pit of the world." There would be times over the next several years when I would agree with his assessment, but not always.

I had been notified by the sheriff's office of a burglary in an area of Hollis known as the "flats." It was a poor area of town on the south side, primarily made up of African Americans and Hispanics.

The Harmon County Sheriff at the time, was Pete Cunningham. Pete felt one of my clients had committed the burglary and wanted me involved in the investigation. This request was not unusual as officers during those years, were encouraged to assist law enforcement when the opportunity arose. This was especially true in the district I worked. My supervisor, Calvin Vincent, had, at one time, been a county sheriff. He always told us to help other officers because we would need their help, at sometime. That was the most valuable piece of advice Calvin ever gave me.

I interviewed the elderly man who had only recently lost his wife and was still grieving over the loss. He advised that the only thing in the world he had was a box of silverware that had belonged to his late wife. That was the only thing taken in the burglary. As I looked around his home, it was obvious he had nothing of value.

I was incensed at this crime after talking with the old gentleman and watching the tears run down his face. I promised him I would find and return his property.

Along with my firearms training as a youth, my Father also taught me to track, and I was pretty good. It took me only a few minutes to pick up the trail of the person who had taken the old man's property. I followed the signs only a few yards before finding the box of silverware hidden in a patch of weeds. I suspected that the person who took it was going to come back after dark and retrieve his loot.

After returning the property to the victim, I continued to track the suspect across a small field and to the area of the Blue-Front Bar. I was still carrying a trace of anger when I entered the bar looking for a certain individual. You could have heard a pin drop. Not only was I the wrong color, I felt that I was not welcome at the Blue-Front Bar. I knew I was probably in the wrong place at the wrong time, but I wanted the person who robbed the elderly gentleman.

The man I was looking for was not there, but I would catch up with him later.

I walked around inside the bar for a few minutes before going into the back room through a blanket-covered doorway. What I saw in the back room was a total shock. There was a five-gallon jar on a table that contained a human fetus. I estimated the baby was approximately five months along, probably still-born. I did not look long enough to determine the sex or race. To say the least, I was appalled and angry. I just couldn't imagine a good reason for that display.

When I left the bar, I saw a young Highway Patrol Trooper sitting just off the road in front of the bar. He called me over and said, "Paul, we don't even go in there."

Needless to say, the Blue-Front Bar was closed down. I still had some faith in humanity, but I must say, the level had dropped several points from the day before.

I learned later that the owner of the bar was charging his patrons ten-cents to view the jar and its contents. That made things even worse, as far as I was concerned. I believe that was the time in my life when I coined a new phrase that would be with me many years, "Most people should be shot."

LOCKED REFRIGERATOR

Many of the elderly people, especially those of African American descent, lived in poverty in Hollis. As one of the most deprived counties in Oklahoma, it was something that was difficult for me. Some of those people wondered where their next meal was coming from.

Having been to several houses in Hollis, searching for a young black man, I finally found his mother's home. It was difficult to locate a particular address in the "flats" in Hollis, because house numbers were not accurate. Many did not have house numbers, but the ones that did, were usually incorrect. There could be the same number on several houses, even in different blocks. A person actually has to know the people to find anyone.

I knocked on the front door, but quickly stepped back; the inside of the screen door was covered with flies. It was so bad, I could not see through the screen. "Come in," I heard someone say. I stepped to one side, opened the screen door as thousands of flies escaped from the residence. When I was certain all the flies had gone, I went into the house. My invitation into the house had come from a heavy-set black women sitting in a chair in the living room, with half a watermelon in her lap. All the flies had not escaped; she was covered with them. They were in her hair, all over her front, arms and covered the watermelon she was eating.

The next thing I noticed was a heavy log chain, padlocked and draped around the refrigeration. I'm talking about a chain with four-inch links capable of pulling tons. The padlock was huge, probably six-inches long.

The woman did have a son on probation, but he was working in the cotton fields. When asked about the heavy chain, she said it was necessary to keep her children from stealing her food. I told her I would come back later and left.

I couldn't help feeling sorry for this woman and her family. A patterned lifestyle that has gone on for years, is extremely difficult to break. It simply becomes a way of life for some people; that is the only thing they know.

MCKNIGHT, OKLAHOMA

Although the town of Mcknight, Oklahoma has all but disappeared, at one time it was a thriving community approximately five miles north of Hollis.

In 1889, Edward Harmon McKnight moved his family from Mississippi to Greer County Texas where he established a farming operation. When the Oklahoma Territory was established, the United States Congress transferred Greer County from Texas to Oklahoma. Sometime later, the county of Harmon was created from the southern part of Greer County, named after Edward Harmon McKnight. The McKnight Settlement was near Mr. McKnight's store he had established.

In the early part of my career as an officer, I received a call from Harmon County Sheriff Pete Cunningham advising me of a robbery and shooting at the McKnight store. Pete said there were four Mexicans who robbed the elderly store keeper and shot her for no reason. Although she survived the attack, she was in serious condition.

I could tell from Pete's voice he was extremely upset. He said at least one of the suspects was going to be on my caseload.

I was in Hollis within an hour and began assisting law enforcement in locating the suspects. It wasn't long before I was advised that three of the four men had been taken into custody. The shooter (my client) was still at large.

I supervised a young Mexican man who was in the country illegally. He had witnessed another of my clients jump on the back of another man and cut his throat. I needed the man as a witness in the case.

Because the United States Immigration Authorities were

making regular sweeps through Harmon County in search of illegals, I moved my witness out in the county in an effort to keep him from being returned to Mexico. I know what you're thinking, but I didn't have much choice; I needed the other client off the streets.

Things had been so bad in Harmon County with illegals that INS was there almost every week. They were rounding up families and returning them to Mexico which was beginning to cause some county work-force problems.

The Cotton Growers Association in the county had contacted me making a strange request. They asked that I try to get the State of Oklahoma to provide me with a different vehicle. I had never really thought about it, but the Dodge vehicle I was driving was painted "Border Patrol Green" with a couple of antennas on the back for state radios. The Association advised, "Every time you come into town, we have to shut the cotton gin down because all our workers think you are the Border Patrol." How funny is that? I did get another vehicle.

But back to my story. I made contact with the client I was trying to "hide," in hopes of developing some information. At the time, he was working at the cotton gin in the press-room. When I made contact, he became very quiet and subdued, which was unlike his normal demeanor. I could sense something was not right and simply left the compress room, returning to the sheriff's office. It was only a few minutes before he called to advise: "The man you are looking for was hiding behind a pile of bagging in the press-room holding a lead pipe. I was afraid to say anything because I thought he might hit you with the pipe. If you will wait about 15 minutes, he is leaving in a truck as a passenger. He will be playing snooker at the pool hall down town. He should be on the first table as you walk in and will be wearing a black shirt and blue pants."

I had never received such a description or details on a person's movements. If this worked out, we would have all the individuals involved in the robbery and shooting.

I quickly picked up an off-duty Oklahoma Highway Patrol Trooper and we walked into the pool hall down-town Hollis. Most of the establishment's customers were running out the back door by the time we spotted the suspect. He was wearing a black shirt and blue pants, playing on the first table. It was almost too good to be true.

Knowing he was caught, he dropped his pool queue and put both hands on the table. Within a few minutes, we had the man in restraints and were walking into the sheriff's office. After one look at Pete, I knew he was mad as hell. I didn't know what he might do.

We had just entered the office with the suspect when Pete grabbed him, shoving him in a corner of the room. Pete drew his old .38 pistol and shoved the barrel against the man's forehead. All the time, Pete was shouting, "Talk you son-of-a-bitch, talk!" We watched in horror as he cocked the hammer. Pete was shaking so bad, we could hear the old pistol rattling – it had been worn out for years. I remember considering putting my fingers in my ears, thinking the old pistol would go off at any minute. The Mexican was also giving it up, but in Spanish. No one could understand a word he was saying.

To our amazement, Pete put his gun down and stepped back. I think he had simply lost control of the situation, but had regained his composure.

Needless to say, we were all glad it was over. All the men were convicted and sent to prison for a very long time. My witness is still in the Hollis area, has raised his family, retired and is now a US Citizen. Some things do work out, even if I did "bend" the law slightly.

BO AND LUKE

Working as an officer in those days, was not all doom and gloom. There were many moments when we actually had fun and enjoyed the job. It seems to me, that more time was spent getting together with our families at special times, events, picnics, etc.

There has always been a special bond between myself and Eugene Hopper, who was an officer for many years. We usually relied on each other when there were problems, but, more importantly, we always stayed in touch, even when distance separated us.

Early in our careers, we were together on our way back from some type of law enforcement function in northern Oklahoma. Eugene was driving, which was a hazard in itself, and I was the sleeping passenger. I don't mean to say he was a bad driver, but he sometimes simply didn't pay attention to what he was doing and always drove fast. That night was one of those times.

We arrived at an intersection, not your normal junction but a "T." The direction we were traveling took us to the end of the pavement, requiring that we go right or left, not straight on where there was only a pasture and fence. We were traveling at Eugene's normal speed (around 75 or 80) when we arrived at the end of the road. I suddenly heard the engine race and had the sensation of flying through the air. My feelings were correct; we were flying through the air.

I know it sounds crazy, but it was a good thing we were traveling at a high speed; it helped us completely clear a five-wire fence and into a pasture. I felt like Bo and Luke Duke of the "Dukes of Hazard," flying through the air in the "General Lee." The landing wasn't bad, since we were both still alive, no thanks to Eugene. When we were certain of our dead-or-alive status, we found a gate and were on the highway again, this time, with a healthy respect for Oklahoma highways and intersections, especially the dead-ends.

Our report to the department included a notation regarding a stray cow in the middle of the highway, causing us to swerve off the road. The vehicle sustained only minor damage (it was a miracle) thanks to Eugene's marvelous driving skills in avoiding the large cow. That was our story and we stuck to it.

GLEN HOOPER

Eugene worked for several years with the Department of Corrections before transferring to the Oklahoma Department of Public Safety Highway Patrol Division. He worked for approximately 15 years before returning to Probation and Parole .

Eugene Hopper would become known to many within the Department of Corrections, and other departments and agencies, as Glen Hooper.

Early in my career with the department, and as Eugene and I began to work together, I began addressing him as "Glen Hooper," as a joke. The name caught on, and before long, he began to receive mail addressed with that name, as well as, training records, court records, etc.

Sometimes, we start things that last a lifetime. We need to take care in what we do and what we say.

A CLOUD OF DUST AND A BENT FRAME

When I started working as a field officer, most of us drove our personal vehicles, collecting mileage from the state. As time and money permitted, the department began to purchase a few vehicles for their officers. We also leased state motor pool cars at various times.

I was assigned a motor pool vehicle, at that particular time, and it was the best state vehicle I have ever driven; it was a Ford Torino.

On my way home from Mangum in the afternoon, I received a broadcast that two inmates had escaped from the Oklahoma State Reformatory in a state pickup. I was almost to the river bridge north of town when I saw the pickup pulling off the highway onto a dirt road. The county road ran west from the river bridge.

I began chasing the pickup down the dirt road, but the heavy dust made it almost impossible to stay close to them. As the visibility was beginning to get somewhat better, I could see an irrigation ditch across the road. Because of my speed, I was unable to stop. It was the Dukes of Hazard all over again as the engine roared and the Ford Torino left the ground like a rocket blasting into space. When I was across the ditch, the front bumper was the first thing that struck the ground. It was a sudden stop, with my briefcase, from the back seat, striking me in the back of the head. Both sun visors slapped the windshield as dust started to settled from the headliner.

The inmates didn't fair any better, and were apprehended. When I surveyed the damage, I was shocked. There was a slight crease across the hood of my vehicle, indicating a bent frame. When I backed up to take a better look, it was obvious that the Ford's frame was severely bent. It resembled a banana split bowl. I knew it was ruined. This old car had survived some hard running and a collision with the courthouse, but not the irrigation ditch.

Yes, I did run into the Greer County Courthouse when the Sheriff's Office was located on the north side on the first floor. The Torino had a bumper and grill that came to a point, however, I have no excuse for the collision. I pulled into the parking lot one day, and simply ran into the side of the courthouse. I just wasn't paying attention to what I was doing. The car survived but I think I knocked a few bricks loose.

I called the motor pool, following the short pursuit, advising of the vehicle's condition. I was able to drive it to Oklahoma City, although I could not travel over 40 mph. I can't remember the replacement, but I know it was nothing like the Ford.

I don't know if there is a moral to this story or not. Perhaps I learned not to run in the dust, unable to see - maybe not.

THE DOG MAN

Everyone who had been around the prison system in Southwest Oklahoma knew the "dog-man." He was an inmate at the Oklahoma State Reformatory serving 99 years for killing a man in a bar fight. He was what the system called "a good inmate." He never caused any problems and was the person who maintained the old antiquated doors in the west cell house. He also worked with the dog handler, giving the dogs a run for their money. In other words, he was the test case for the practicing dogs.

After serving at least 12 years of his sentence, he was paroled. He had no family he wished to reunite with and finally chose to remain in Mangum, which is 13 miles from the prison in Granite.

Because of his work record in prison, he had no trouble getting a job with a rock quarry near Granite.

He immediately began to experience some adjustment problems, primarily because of other black men where he lived. Some were giving him a hard time, causing him to fear for his life. I tried to assist the man with adjustment problems, but his fear finally caused him to violate his parole.

I received information that he was carrying a handgun for protection, which is considered an automatic return to prison, especially considering his crime. I made contact with him and found that he was wearing a shoulder holster containing a .32 caliber pistol. I remember laughing at the sight of the weapon, making the comment that I was going save his life and take the pistol from him. In fact, I think both of us were laughing before the contact was over. I know what you are thinking. You think this was a serious situation and it was not funny. Wrong.

Allow me to explain. As I recall, the .32 caliber pistol was a nickel-plated RG. This particular company makes some of the cheapest pistols I have ever seen. Instead of screws, it was pinned together and was made of the cheapest pot-metal I had ever seen. I would never allow them on the range when I was instructing, nor did Probation and Parole allow an officer to carry one as a duty weapon. Even in proper working order, there was a good chance they would blow up.

This particular weapon was missing the trigger and all the components required to rotate and lock the cylinder in place. The only working part was the hammer and the only way to fire the pistol was to put a shell in the cylinder, line it up with the barrel (the best you could) pull the hammer back and let it go. More than likely, it would have blown up in his face causing major injuries or death. It was about the most dangerous thing I had seen anyone actually carrying. It would have been a real "stretch" to label it a weapon.

Another "bending" of the rules. I thought I could see some potential in this man. He had not threatened or injured anyone; the pistol he had was more of a piece of junk than a weapon, (although it was legally, a firearm) and I thought he deserved another chance.

I did write a report but I did not request parole revocation.

Today, that man owns several rent houses in Mangum, is married, his wife has a business and he has retired. I'll never regret giving him another chance. He is also my friend.

There was one thing I learned from my first supervisor, Calvin Vincent, "You just have to use common sense when you're dealing with these people."

PRISON TRACKING DOGS

It has been said that you can take everything away from a person and he or she will rebel in some way. But, if you deprive an individual of their freedom, they will not rest until they have regained it.

Our great country was founded because liberties and freedoms had been taken away in another country. Many of our countrymen have given their lives for the American way of life – freedom. A human being was not meant to live without that precious gift, however, in our society, our laws are designed to protect the innocent and it is necessary that those who prey on others, pay the price. That often means taking away a person's freedom.

Prison escapes occur for a variety of reasons: an inmate fears for his life; loneliness for family or loved ones; or simply a spur of the moment decision. For whatever reason, it happens frequently.

I remember searching for two young men one morning following their escape from the Oklahoma State Reformatory. They were missed at one of the prison's headcounts. I'm not sure how they managed to escape.

An Oklahoma Highway Patrol Trooper had captured one of the men and medical personnel were busy picking shotgun pellets out of the young fugitive. The other man was still on the run.

I was driving south on a state highway about eight miles from the prison when the other escapee walked out of an irrigation canal. I could see the numbers on his blue denim shirt. I could also see that he was no more than 20 years old.

I pulled off the road and began a foot pursuit. My initial

problem was the mud I collected on my boots as I crossed the irrigation ditch. That slowed me down a great deal, however, I gained on the young man for the first couple of hundred yards. But due to his age (and mine) he slowly began to increase the distance between us. That was when I decided to try and slow him down. I fired a shot from my sidearm striking a tree a few yards ahead of the man.

He stopped in his tracks, slowly turned around and looked at me from a hundred yards away. I was waving at him to come back. I could almost see the wheels turning in his head as he weighed his chances. A moment later, he was running again, but this time, in a serpentine pattern which allowed me to gain on him again. He didn't know it at the time, but I had no intention of firing on him. We were in an open field, he had no weapon (that I could see) and he was not going to get away. There were other officers in the area who would soon be arriving to assist.

Almost anything has its downside. I was gaining on the young man, but I could hear the tracking dogs behind me. The dog handler had turned them out behind me. I didn't think that was very bright on his part, however, a confrontation would have to wait. My immediate thought was what I would do to avoid having to shoot the department's dogs.

A cross-fence running through the field answered my prayers, while saving the dogs. I found a nice round post and climbed the fence, standing on top of the post. The dogs made one circle around the post before picking up the trail of the escapee. Once they were solidly on the trail again, I followed them watching as they "treed" the young escapee in a Mesquite tree. When I arrived, he had climbed as high as possible and was gently swaying from side to side in the light breeze.

Our conversation, before other officers arrived, hinged on the man's belief that I would not have shot him. I asked why he had not given up after I fired a shot near him. His reply was, "I just didn't think you would shoot me." There was no need to question his somewhat flawed reasoning. Instead, I pointed out that, at least he didn't have a butt full of lead like his partner.

I have always been thankful for the good, solid fence post.

MONTICELLO, MISSISSIPPI

Linda and I were still living on the farm when this young man appeared on my caseload. Originally from Mississippi, he had committed an armed robbery in Oklahoma and after serving a rather lengthy prison term at the Oklahoma State Reformatory, was released on parole.

While in prison, he met and was mentored by a psychologist who worked at the prison. Once he was released on parole, he remained in Greer County under my supervision.

He began very well, although he was borderline mentally retarded. Living on the streets most of his life had given him general knowledge, or what we refer to as being "street wise" – at least enough to get by. He was capable of holding a job, taking care of himself and managing his money with only minimal assistance.

His problems began when he met a young women in the Granite area who was retarded to the extent of not being able to care for herself. She lived with her parents when she was not in a state facility. I talked with him several times, warning him not to see this woman anymore. Although I was supported by her parents, the psychologist would secretly help them see one another, and before long my worst nightmares were realized. The young woman was pregnant.

The psychologist, who was also a preacher, married them and they were soon living together, against my wishes and the wishes of her parents.

I had previously cautioned this young man not to come to my home. I had two small daughters who I had always attempted to shield from my work and the people on my caseload. After the second time he came to my home, I advised him I would place him in jail if he returned.

Some people listen to what you are saying, but it just doesn't seem to make an impression. That was true with this client. He showed up at my home only a few days after I had warned him. I searched his vehicle and arrested him. He was carrying several weapons in his vehicle: a baseball bat with steel spikes driven into the wood, a knife and a chain (clearly not used to pull things.)

All the way to the county jail, he asked what charge I had arrested him on. By the time we arrived in Mangum, I had decided on an offense of disturbing the peace and possession of deadly weapons. He promised he would return to Mississippi (without the young girl he had married) if I would release him. I agreed and released him.

Within a few days, I was preparing transfer documents for this individual to the state of Mississippi. He had agreed not to leave Oklahoma until his transfer to Mississippi had been approved. He had also agreed not to be with the woman he had married.

It was only a matter of hours before I received a call from the parents of the young woman the offender had married. They advised that my client had attempted to kill their daughter by choking her, kicking her, then throwing her outside in the snow.

I contacted the parolee at a small house near Granite where he had been living. Apparently, he had ordered the young girl to fry chicken after he had heated the oil then placed cut-up pieces in a skillet. She simply stood in front of the stove watching the chicken burn to a crisp. This angered her husband to the point that he assaulted her.

I arrested the man, placed him in a holding cell at the Granite Police Department, and he, again, agreed to return to Mississippi without the young woman. Against my better judgment, I again released him.

This time, he did leave town, but picked up his retarded wife on his way out.

After locating the man in only a few days, I immediately requested a parole revocation warrant from the Oklahoma Department of Corrections. As many of these people do, he had returned to his home state of Mississippi where he was raised. It did not take long for the local sheriff to arrest the man, placing a detainer on him for Oklahoma.

Over the years, the Department of Corrections contracted with security transport companies to return parolees to Oklahoma from other states. Then, at other times, we transported them ourselves. This was one of those "We go get them" times, and I was on my way to Mississippi.

It took two days to travel to Monticello, Mississippi where my prisoner was being held. What I remember most about my initial arrival, was the outdoor jail. As I stopped in front of the county courthouse, I could see a strap-iron cage sitting out in the yard under a giant oak tree. When the parolee saw me, he shouted, "Mr. Morris, get me the hell out of here." I later asked what happened when it rained, to which he replied, "You get wet."

The man was returned to Oklahoma, provided a preliminary parole revocation hearing, then returned to prison. His wife would later give birth to a boy, who was also extremely retarded. After several years, he was placed in a group home after it was determined that he was more mentally challenged than either of his parents. He was unable to complete a full, spoken sentence. He will require constant care the rest of his life.

Years later and after this individual had been released from prison, I received a telephone call from the Mississippi Bureau of Investigation. They asked that I attempt to locate the man, arrest him, then notify authorities in Mississippi. Agents said they were pursuing him as a suspect in the strangulation deaths of three of his young cousins in Mississippi. They had been found in shallow graves.

I located an oil drilling company in Beckham county where I learned I had missed the man by two days. Authorities would later find my former client in California, return him to Mississippi, where he was convicted in the three homicides. He was sentenced to three life sentences.

I often think of the lives lost in this case and the damage done to so many others. It was a very sad situation that could have been avoided if certain people had acted responsibly.

TORNADO ALLEY

If you have never heard the term "Tornado Alley," then you are not from around my neck-of-the-woods. If you have never witnessed a tornado - the most violent and destructive freak of nature - then you, obviously, don't live in Southwest Oklahoma. If you have never heard either of these terms, then you have lived most of your life under a rock.

I don't suppose any part of the United States is free from tornados, but the area of Texas, north through Oklahoma, Kansas, Missouri, Nebraska and South Dakota, make up what is commonly known as "Tornado Alley."

Tornadoes are more likely to develop during the warm, spring and summer months, averaging around 800 each year in the United States. From those storms, an average of 80 people lose their lives and 1500 are injured each year. The property damage would be difficult to estimate.

Only about two-percent of tornadoes are extremely violent - by that, I mean with winds in the neighborhood of 250 mph. Such a storm can develop a damage path of one mile wide, traveling some 50 miles. Several of these have come through Oklahoma during my lifetime.

I don't remember the first tornado I ever witnessed, but I do recall some of the more memorable ones in the State of Oklahoma.

Linda and I were still farming and both employed away from the farm. I remember the storm that began in the southwest before moving across our farm. The old house we lived in was no more than a shell when Shannon was a child.

The "wall front" preceding the tornado was black as the night with a drastic change in temperature. It began to hail, and I do mean hail. Although only a few, they were the size of softballs. We could hear them coming through the air, causing a strange sort of whistle. When they hit the ground, the sound was like cannon balls being dropped from an airplane. Luckily, none of them hit our house.

The tornado never hit the ground, but was only a few feet from touching down when it came over our house. It blew one of the back bedroom windows out before taking our television antenna down. The wind was so violent, the carpet rose a foot off the floor.

My next move was one of the dumbest things I have ever done in my life. I wrapped Shannon in a blanket and headed for my parents storm shelter, more than 200 yards away. Linda was trying to keep up as I jumped over fallen trees and dodged flying objects. We all made it to the shelter but could have very easily been killed by debris flying through the air. Strange things occur in a man's head when his child is in danger. I was certainly not thinking straight that day.

I was working in Sayre one day when a storm front hit the area. I was assisting the Beckham County Sheriff's Department search for an escaped prisoner who had vaulted over the dispatch desk, then alluded officers.

I was in my vehicle sitting across the river, watching the area for the escapee. Approximately 200 yards east of where I was, Beckham County Deputy, Danny Garza, a good friend, sat in his vehicle. I saw a small "twister" (an Okie term for a tornado) in the air, but it did not appear to be on the ground. At about the same time, Danny's voice came over my police radio, "Dispatch, what does a tornado look like?" He had just finished his question when I noticed the rope-like tail of the tornado, 50 yards from where Danny and I were. The tail whipped back and forth, throwing debris in all directions. I quickly advised Danny that he was indeed looking at a tornado. We didn't hang around.

The tornado was only a small one, but could have easily flipped a vehicle causing injury.

I recall another instance when I was storm-spotting with Dale Rogers, Chief of Police in Mangum. There was a tornado spotted east of Mangum but its movement could not be verified (although they generally move from southwest to northeast).

We had chased the twister several miles, losing it in the heavy rain, hail and dark clouds. We stopped on a paved road east of town in an effort to get a better view of the clouds from outside our vehicle. As I looked up, the center of the twister was just above me. Luckily, it did not decide to put down while I stood there staring into the most power weather phenomena on earth. Needless to say, we moved along rather quickly.

COMO SE LLAMA USTED?

I have always enjoyed traveling across desert, although during most of the year, it is hotter than a depot stove (or as my friend would say, "hotter that a kitten in a wool basket.") The beauty and tranquility of the wide-open spaces is relaxing - at least for me.

Interstate 40 divided a portion of the area I worked, winding through Custer and Beckham Counties. It has always been a route for drug smugglers, illegal aliens and everything imaginable. A person could see almost anything on this famous highway, from men carrying crosses to others walking, hitch hiking, begging for food, gas, clothing - you name it and they were after it.

It was common to see Mexicans walking I-40, many of whom were seeking work to support their families back in Mexico. With only a minimal amount of training, it is not uncommon to spot dozens of suspected illegals traveling by pickups, campers, vans, trucks and older vehicles. One can only imagine the amount of illegal drugs traveling our great interstates.

Deputy Danny Garza, who didn't know about tornadoes, happened to be in the Beckham County Sheriff's office the day two suspected Mexican Nationals were brought in for investigation. Since the officer was obviously of Mexican descent, we all assumed he could speak Spanish. Because the suspected illegals had no identification on them, we asked Danny to go into the interrogation room and get their names.

You should know how intimidating this deputy was. He stood at approximately 6', and weighed around 300 lbs. He could usually stop a bar fight by simply showing up.

He walked into the interrogation room, stood over the two men pointing his finger at them as he asked, "What ..... Is ..... your....name?" With no response, he became somewhat agitated as he again asked, "I …said….what…..is……your…..name?"

By this time, we were all laughing our heads off, to the point of losing our breath. We stopped Danny before he hurt one of the men. When asked if he could speak Spanish, he replied, "Well, hell no; I was born in Germany!" That statement really broke us up. I remember tears running down my checks while I laughed for several minutes. When we determined that he had experienced enough "good fun," we all stopped. After all, he could have probably whipped all of us at the same time.

Things are not always as they seem, but what a good laugh.

COMO SE LLAMA USTED? DONDE VIVA USTED? ALTO! ALTO!

It was always comforting to have a partner, especially when working the oil boom in the early 70's in Beckham County. I was fortunate in that the Department of Corrections had hired Harlan Ross, sending him my way. Harlan had a degree in psychology, was a good shot and a former Marine. That's all I needed to know. Although he was new to the job, he had common sense in addition to experience in law enforcement. His ability to identify one of his clients, however, was not so good on a particular day.

We were in my vehicle traveling to Clinton on Interstate 40 east, when my new partner spotted a hitchhiker on the other side of the interstate. I will attempt to relay to you the exact conversation that ensued.

"Hey, see that guy over there?"

"Yes, what about him?"

"I have a warrant for his arrest."

"No you don't. How can you even see who he is from here?"

"No, really, I have a warrant for that man!"

"Alright Harlan, but you better be right."

From that point, I slowed, crossed the median and approached the man as I pulled off the roadway.

We started walking toward the man, after stopping our vehicle. He turned toward us, while walked backward, then, put both of his hands behind him and into his backpack.

I had held up my badge, but after he would not stop and the fact that he had both hands in his backpack, I drew my weapon. When he saw the gun, he threw the backpack to the ground, ran over to the guard rail, grabbing it with both hands. He had done that before.

At that point in the sideshow, my partner announced, "That's not my man."

The only reason I didn't shoot my new partner was that I had new bullets in my weapon, he had a wife and a young daughter I was fond of, and I really needed help.

So what did we do from that point? I dumped his pack on the ground, stirred through his few, meager possessions and after finding no weapons, put everything back and told him to go. As I waved in the direction he had been walking, assuring him everything was alright, he slightly nodded at me before walking on.

How would I have explained that shooting to my boss?

The lesson: Not everyone walking the interstate is wanted, and Harlan needed a stronger prescription for his glasses.

AS BAD AS IT GETS

I have been in some filthy homes, but this one would take the prize for the century.

I was working in the Elk City area during the time when the oil fields were extremely active. It was during a period of time when housing was in short supply, with people living in anything that provided a roof over their heads, regardless of the cost or condition. I have seen workers living under bridges, in storm shelters, in a tree house, cars, and tents. Many locations provided very little shelter. It was simply a time of chaos.

Trying to locate someone who had transferred into Elk City from another state, was a daily routine. The addresses I was given, would often be several weeks old and the people had moved several times. I would estimate a third of my time was exhausted searching for individuals.

I don't remember the families name, but I do remember the house. I had driven by it several times, thinking it was abandoned as there were no vehicles or other signs of life. The weeds had grown up around the structure giving it the appearance of an old house unfit to live in - that was actually the case.

After checking the front door, I was greeted by a young child who invited me into the living room - I think it was the living room. An older man, appeared in a doorway on the other side of the room, flipping a light switch as he pulled his shirt over his head. The smell was that of a garbage dump, but even worse, were the thousands of cockroaches that appeared with the light, then just as quickly, disappeared.

The man was not the person I was searching for, but something had to be done about the living situation because of the two young children residing in the home.

There was a cage in the kitchen area containing ferrets. As a slid the cage to one side with my foot, I found maggots in the carpet. I called the police department, who, after looking at the house, called the Health Department. We gave the people a few minutes to remove only minimal items from the structure, then called the fire department, who burned the place to the ground. It was simply a place not fit for human beings, much less, a child.

A LESSON IN CURSING

I believe it was in the early 1970s while we were still living on the farm, that a man came to my house one day. He advised me of a woman living at the foot of the Wichita Mountains on the northwest side of Mt. Walsh. He claimed she was a parole violator, having been in prison for killing her husband with a shotgun. He gave me her name, date of birth and other vital information, including the fact that she was on a life sentence when released on parole several years before. When I asked why he was providing me with the information, he simply said he had lived with her in the past but was not getting along with her now. I quickly developed a dislike for the man. What he was telling me would return her to confinement for the rest of her life. I would have to hate someone a great deal to do that, I thought.

The next day, I ran the information through NCIC, discovering the woman had been a fugitive for several years following her release on parole. She had never reported to a Probation and Parole officer.

For the next several days, I attempted to locate the woman, but she was never at home. Something wasn't right.

A few days later, the man who had given me the information, simply walked into my living room. He didn't knock, ring the doorbell or say a word. My wife shouted at me telling me about the intruder. I ran into the living room seeing a man standing in the doorway. I tackled him and we both rolled down the front steps of our house as he shouted, "I was just going to tell you something."

After I explained breaking and entering or being shot inside someone's home, he advised me that the woman I was searching for knew I was looking for her. She was staying in the house during the night, and was hiding in the mountains during the day, under an old tarp. Late at night, she would return to the house.

I contacted Eugene Hopper, a good friend of mine. He was an Officer in Clinton, but lived only a short distance from me. That night, about midnight, or later, we went to her house, knocked on the door, then announced who we were. Of course the door was locked, but we could hear the woman inside the bedroom trying to encourage her dogs to attack us. Her pronunciation of words, indicated she was probably drunk. After some time, and as she would not answer or come to the door, I began kicking the door in. Eugene went to the back door and checked it, finding it unlocked. He laughingly advised me of the way into the house. I would find out later that she had nailed several 2 x 4s over the front door. I would be there kicking on the front door today, had the back door not been unlocked. Also, my partner has never let me forget about the door.

As we entered the house, we walked through the living room then into the bedroom where we found her, drunk, without clothing of any kind. Also, before entering the bedroom, and just at the doorway, there was a 12" butcher knife on top of the television set. I pushed it back until it fell behind the television set.

After we got her out of bed and made her put some clothes on, we advised her of the charge and warrant. She was less than impressed. As we walked her out of the bedroom, she reached for the knife on the television. When she determined that it was no longer there, she became very agitated and vocal, even for a drunk.

Almost immediately, she began to curse and didn't let up until we arrived at the Beckham County Jail in Sayre. At that particular time, Greer County would not hold women prisoners.

All the way to Sayre, she expounded on my ancestry, Eugene's ancestry and everything in between. At one point, she did stop briefly and asked, "Paul (we were now on a first name basis) does your wife know where you are?" When I said yes, she only laughed and began to curse again. I had never heard such language, especially from a woman. She certainly gave us a lesson in cursing that night, although we could have done just as well without it.

To further show her stubbornness at her parole revocation hearing, she was offered an opportunity to go to substance abuse treatment and remain on parole status. She said, "Hell no, I'm not going to stop drinking, just send me back to prison."

There was no choice for the hearing officer.

"HE WENT OUT THE BACK DOOR."

Rarely, did I ever enter someone's home without being invited, but on this particular day, there would be an exception.

I was in Sayre, Oklahoma, just trying to find some of my clients at home, when I saw a young man walking in the residential area who was wanted on a Beckham County warrant. He was also one of my probationers.

I pulled over and stopped just as he glanced around at me. Before I could get a word out of my mouth, he was running. I shouted for him to stop, but that just seemed to add speed to his pace. I began to chase him through the residential area until he came to a home and simply ran through the front door. I was a couple of seconds behind him and followed him into the house. There was an old gentleman sitting in an easy chair watching television and his wife was knitting. He barely glanced at me and said, "He went out the back door." I don't think his wife even looked up. It seemed almost funny at the time that neither of them seemed to mind the extra company.

As I ran out the back door, I discovered only an open field and a storm shelter with an open door. I had called the sheriff's department before the foot pursuit, and I could now hear a siren coming my way.

Knowing the man was probably in the storm shelter, I waited for another officer.

The Beckham County Sheriff slid to a stop in front of the house. He appeared from the corner of the house in a gentle jog asking where the man had gone. I quickly explained the situation.

We called for the man to come out of the cellar, but there was no sound. Finally, in an effort to get the man to give up, the sheriff shouted, "Give me that shotgun. I'm going to fire off a couple of shots down there. He'll come out."

There was no pause or wasted time, the man shouted, "Don't shoot, I'm coming out. Don't shoot, don't shoot."

The sheriff took the prisoner while I apologized to the old couple in the house. They didn't seem to mind, asking if I caught the man. In fact, as I recall, they were both smiling when I talked with them. I think they rather enjoyed the excitement. I hope I never get that bored.

HAND GRENADES AND PIGS

Raising hogs was something I had grown up with. Father always had a few, and we usually had a smoke house where we cured our own meat. I remember "hog butchering" in the fall months of the year when we would kill the hogs, boil them in a cast iron kettle and scrap the hides until they were free of hair. We used every part of the animal; nothing was wasted. I was actually too young to be of much help, but I didn't enjoy the process. It always seemed somewhat cruel to me.

But on a certain night in Mangum, I would learn something about raising hogs.

I thought, by that time in my career, I had seen almost everything; but I was wrong. The Chief of Police in Mangum, Dale Rogers, had asked for my assistance in locating a hand grenade. He and his officers suspected that a certain young man had one at his grandmother's home in Mangum. They asked if I would search the house since the owner was a probationer. Feeling somewhat tentative about the task, I agreed to help.

It was late in the evening when I contacted the boy's grandmother, telling her what I wanted to do. She denied having the hand grenade in her house but said I could search if I wanted. Her statement to me that the house was in somewhat of a mess was an understatement. I should have taken her word.

I began my search in the kitchen where I found some type of beans sprouted around the baseboards. That was nothing new as I had seen much worse. There was mold, filth, dirt and mud on the floors, but that didn't bother me. But what awaited me in the back bedroom, I had never seen.

I made it though the kitchen, living room and started on one of the bedrooms when I detected an odor which I recognized - swine. A normal person could have detected the smell upon entering the house, but I had inherited my Father's poor smelling ability. In fact, he had told me that he had trapped and skinned skunks for their hides when he was a boy. I always thought I could smell somewhat better than that, but my olvactories did not function properly.

When I looked inside the other bedroom, I found the source of the smell. I found a pig weighing around 250 pounds. My client was in the process (well into the process) of raising a hog in her back bedroom. It was very easy to see that the pig had been there for several months.

I never found the allusive hand grenade and didn't really care. Half way through the search, my desire for fresh air became almost overwhelming.

I am not one to hold a grudge, but I often think about the subtle request made by the Chief of Police and wonder if he had some idea of what was in the house.

Oh well, at least I didn't get my head blown off. I just considered myself lucky, but couldn't wait to get home and take a much needed shower. No more pork chops or bacon for a while.

MOVING FROM THE FARM

In the mid 1970s, Linda and I decided to stop farming, leave the country and move to Granite. The advantages for our family simply outweighed my desire to remain in the country, so we were faced with leaving our newly remodeled home or trying to move it. I began to search for house movers who possessed the skill and equipment to relocate our home without destroying it.

I contacted Barnes House Movers in Hollis regarding the cost of moving our house as well as checking the type of equipment they used. When I was in their office, I noticed a photograph on the wall that convinced me I had found the company for the job. The photo showed the movers relocating a cement swimming pool. With numerous steel bands and other bracing, the strange looking concrete shell was moved without serious damage. That convinced me.

After purchasing a corner lot on the west side of Granite, I requested Barnes build the foundation for the house. I wanted them to be responsible for the correct fit of the house.

I had several days of preparation before the house could be moved to a paved road over a mile away. From that location, the distance to its new location in Granite, was 12 miles of paved roads.

The trees and narrow road would make it impossible to move without going through pastures and fields. In order to take the structure to a surfaced road, I would be required to cut gaps from shelterbelts. Fences, mail boxes, and other obstacles would have to be moved to accommodate the 60 feet required to move the house.

After a few days with a chain saw, I was ready for the move. Barnes had prepared the foundation, I had moved dirt on the lot in an attempt to level it as much as possible, and I had borrowed extra equipment to pull the house through a mile of deep sand.

The big day was here; I was scared to death. Although Barnes and Company were bonded with a great record, dropping that house would probably destroy it. As much money as we had spent remodeling it, Linda and I were almost in shock when we saw the house suddenly rise in the air. Barnes had a very sophisticated hydraulic system; they cut the pipes loose, set their system up and pushed a button. The entire house rose like a ghost, but evenly.

The crew quickly banded part of the house, slid the steel beams under the structure, hooked up the trucks and advised they were ready to move. I was having second thoughts.

My heart was pounding like a trip-hammer as the trucks started forward, only to sink in the loose sand. We began hooking up equipment to Barnes' truck, starting with a four-wheel drive farm tractor I had borrowed from a friend. The next item was one of the counties road maintainers, operated by a county worker. On the second attempt, the strange caravan of implements followed up by a rather large house, began to move. Once we were moving, we continued across the pastures and fields until we reached the paved road more than a mile south. With our daylight almost gone, we stopped until the following day.

Thank God for paved roads. The distance to Granite would now be easier to cover. At sunrise, I began repairing fences, replacing mailboxes, and driving ahead of the movers, removing any obstacles that would slow the move.

Before I could finish with repairs to fences, signs and mail boxes from the day before, Barnes and his crew were easing our house down on the foundation in Granite. It fit perfectly, but as important, was the relief I felt after seeing our home in one piece.

When we started the move, we were told not to worry about anything in the house. We left the dishes in the cabinets, clothes in closets, tables and chairs remained as they were; I think the only items we secured were suspended lights which were taken down. There was even a glass of water left on the kitchen cabinet which survived the move without moving. The only damage was a crack in the sheetrock ceiling inside one of our closets. Barnes and Company had performed a remarkable feat.

In relocating to Granite, the house faced a different direction than when it was on the farm. I have to admit, for several months, when I would leave the living room to go into a different room, I sometimes walked in the wrong direction. I think I have finally overcome the problem.

YOU BUTCHERED YOUR HOG WITH WHAT?

I have explained my experiences as a young boy when it was time to butcher hogs. This will be somewhat different.

I was trying to locate a transfer to the Erick, Oklahoma area when I discovered a house in a large, thick grove of trees. It was the general area where my new client was reported to live.

I stopped about 100 yards from the house, got out and was looking around when I suddenly heard a chainsaw spring to life. I'm sure you will agree when I say a chainsaw has a distinctive sound. I followed the sound through the trees, finally locating the source. I was seeing something I had never witnessed. A man was standing in front of a large pig that had ropes around its front feet then pulled up into a tree. The man was wearing a leather or vinyl apron and goggles. The chainsaw revved up and the chain and bar started down through the hog. I have never seen such a mess with meat and blood flying everywhere.

I suppose there are different ways to butcher a hog, but I didn't care for the man's method.

THE UNLUCKY CATTLE THIEF

Cattle are not difficult to steal, especially if there is a good corral and loading chute. But, if a person is the slightest bit unlucky, he might just get caught.

A few years ago, in Greer County, several head of cattle were taken from a ranch north of Granite owned by William and Billy Don Petzold. Also, the same night, a farmer/rancher near Mangum lost his cattle trailer. The two crimes were obviously connected because of the distance separating the thefts and the timing.

Greer County Under Sheriff Tim Scott investigated the crimes and connected them because of an item he found at the location north of Granite. The thief had, apparently, stayed the night before at the Duffer Motel in Mangum. At some point in his activities, the night he stole the cattle, the motel receipt blew out of his vehicle lodging in the side of the cattle chute. How unlucky can a person be, but it was a great find for Tim.

Officer Scott contacted me after he determined the man he was searching for, was under Department of Corrections supervision. He was actually on parole for, guess what crime? Good answer. Yes, it was Larceny of Domestic Animals - cattle. We quickly located him in Eastern Oklahoma.

Before we left Granite that day, William Petzold gave us a rope from his pickup, asking that we save the taxpayers the cost of prosecution when we located the cattle thief. Oh, for the good old days.

In talking with the sheriff, in the county where the parolee lived, we determined that he was suspected of other cattle thefts. The sheriff said he would watch the man until we arrived.

By the time we arrived at the small town in Eastern Oklahoma, our man had been picked up by authorities there. It was a relatively short interview. Because of the evidence Officer Scott had, the man admitted to the crimes. He said he had become scared while taking the cattle, but never offered a reason. He dumped the cattle out before he returned to his home in Eastern Oklahoma. He still had the cattle trailer.

On our way back from Eastern Oklahoma, we actually came by the location where the cattle were stolen. I slowed the vehicle, slightly, as Tim and I glanced at each other and smiled. You simply cannot hang a man these days with all the video cameras around.

I have been told that stealing cattle is much like being a drug addict or alcoholic; it is very hard to give up. Hopefully this man would not get another chance, but the court would make that determination.

YOU FOUND A DEAD POSSUM WHERE?

At the time I was working in Beckham County, one of my parolees, who was on parole from Texas for two homicides, had been caught behind a business in Elk City, late at night, with a sawed-off shotgun in a cloth bag. The Elk City Police Department had some fine officers at the time, but the kid next door could have figured this one out; he meant to rob the place.

My client was arrested and placed in the Beckham County Jail where he was later charged with several felonies. In addition to those charges, I had obtained a Texas State Parole Revocation Warrant for his two life sentences. He was staring at lots of time.

One day when I was in Sayre, I dropped by the sheriff's office and was shocked to see that my client had made trustee status. To make matters worse, he was working outside the jail. I immediately contacted the sheriff advising him of the status of his inmate, further advising him of the time he was facing in the state of Texas. For some reason, I could never understand, he left the man on trustee status. By the next morning, he was gone.

The escapee's father-in-law, who lived in the northwest area of Sayre, was my first contact. I knew the man well enough that there was no problem in receiving permission to search his home. His only statement was, "You can come in but those son-of-bitches with you can't." He was referring to the local police. They, apparently, had some sort of on-going problem.

I entered the home in search of the jail escapee, but it was apparent that he was not there. I did, however, find a dead possum in the living room of the home. I don't mean a "new death," it had been there for some time. The floor of the house was simply rough wood with no other covering or finish. The possum was now only a dried carcass , but one could see by the discoloration of the wood, that it had died there, then remained until it dried up, changing the coloring of the wood. The holes in the floor and roof made it easy for an animal to enter the house, but it was surprising that it had died and remained there. And I thought my sense of smell was bad.

I later tracked the man down in Minnesota through one of his old cellmates in the Huntsville Texas Prison. I advised an FBI Agent who was working in Elk City. He contacted agents in Minnesota. I later learned that 2 agents were checking on the man in a state assistance office in a small town in Minnesota, when the escapee walked in. As one of the FBI Agents asked the receptionist if the subject had been in, the escapee walked up behind them as he said, "My name is ------------." One of the agents turned around and knocked the man to the floor.

Following his arrest by the FBI, he was transported back to Beckham County. I can't say I was happy to see him, but he certainly didn't belong on the streets.

ELK CITY BANK ROBBERY

I have always felt that a person robbing a bank is desperate. After all, the offense brings out the "Feds" better known as the FBI. I don't know how knowledgeable you are when it comes to that agency, but I can tell you from experience, they are good. I have worked with several of them over the years. I would not want them after me.

I was driving south of main street in Elk City one day, when my police radio broadcasted a "bank robbery in progress" at the First National Bank. I was passing through the intersection where that business was located as I glanced at the front of the bank. A man ran out the front door wearing a ski mask, carried a bag of money in his left hand and a handgun in his right. I broke out in goose bumps all over. This was a first for me.

I stopped my vehicle in the street and pursued the man on foot. He started down a side street running east with me only a short distance behind him.

I had my weapon out thinking he would probably take a shot at me at some point. I could not, however, fire on him because there were people on past him in the line of fire. I would only fire in self defense, at that point, I thought.

He began to glance back over his shoulder seeing me behind him, but never offered to fire his weapon. I could not, however, run along side of the brick buildings because I felt he would eventually fire on me. I had to stay close to vehicles parked along the street in case I needed quick cover.

The man was no more than 25 yards from me when he came to the end of the block. I watched as he turning the corner running south. It took me several seconds to turn the corner behind him for safety reasons. I had to make several quick peeks around the corner before continuing the pursuit. By the time I felt it safe to turn the corner, I observed him throw the mask in a dumpster at the south end of the block. By the time I arrived at the dumpster, he had vanished.

It was only a couple of minutes before police arrived. We attempted to seal off the area as best we could, with limited help, then systematically began to search each business and building in the area. After several hours, with no results, we called off the search.

As far as I know, the man was never caught. So, I guess you could say, "Sometimes, crime pays (but not often)." I believe, the FBI has about a 90% solve rate when it comes to bank robberies. Those are not good odds for the bad guy.

GOULD, OKLAHOMA BANK ROBBERY

Gould, Oklahoma is a very small, sleepy little town in Harmon County just about as far southwest as a person can travel without being in Texas. The population of the small farming community is around 200 with a large number of migrant workers.

With a total population of approximately 3200 in the entire county, a bank robbery came as a complete surprise to many. This would be labeled one of the most savage and senseless robberies in Western Oklahoma's history.

Two black men walked into the bank in Gould one day and announced the robbery. One of the male workers was severely pistol whipped and a female teller was kidnapped. She was taken out in the country, where she was murdered.

I remember receiving the bulletin from the Mangum Police Department dispatcher, as all agencies attempted to set up road blocks all over that part of Oklahoma. I was sent to the river bridge south of Granite to assist the Granite Chief of Police on a road block. We were looking for a yellow vehicle containing one or two black males. Officers were putting everything on hold to help with the search. The senseless murder of the young woman, incensed the people in Southwest Oklahoma.

We began to stop vehicles and perform cursory searches, while explaining to people the reason for the road block. Most didn't mind the inconvenience, especially when they learned of the brutal murder. Some went so far as to offer to assist with the search.

I recall the weather being somewhat warm that day, and to make matters worse, we were standing in the sun on asphalt. Suddenly, the chief was summoned back to town due to a disturbance incident. That left me alone on the road block, but we didn't think anything about it.

As the officer raced toward Granite, he called back to advise of meeting a yellow vehicle with several blacks inside. My heart began to race as I saw the vehicle appear on the horizon. I set up and began to wave the vehicle to the side of the road. I half expected them to run through the block, which caused me to load my shotgun with slugs, in case I was forced to take a tire off the vehicle or disable the engine.

To my surprise, they pulled over. I ordered all of them out and laid them out on the pavement while I searched the vehicle. I began to relax when I saw fishing rods and fresh bait in the car. They were also not matching the description I had received earlier. When I found nothing in their vehicle to tie them to the robbery, I allowed them to proceed. After I explained the situation, some of them became more cooperative while others continued to give me a "go-to-hell look." I don't think they enjoyed laying on the hot pavement; I could understand their anger.

Both men were eventually captured and sent to prison. I think one of them was murdered while in custody, which was at least some measure of justice. It was such a senseless crime.

The other thing I can remember about that day was, it was not a good day for a black man to be driving a yellow car.

WHERE IS YOUR PRISONER?

PCP (phencyclidine) was one of the most widely used illegal drugs in the 1960s through the 1980s. Classified as a hallucinogen, it effected different people in different ways, but always negatively. Because of its many faces, it was considered one of the most dangerous drugs on the street. It could be an anesthetic, stimulant, depressant and hallucinogen all at the same time, often causing violent and unpredictable behavior, seizures, coma and death. It could also make a giant out of very small person.

I had just pulled into a parking space at the Elk City Police Department/Fire Department that day. Both Departments shared a common building, in those days.

A friend of mine, who was in his middle 60s and a Beckham County Deputy Sheriff, had only a few seconds before, also parked and was opening his door. While he was getting out of his patrol unit, I noticed the passenger-side door fly open and a person sort of fall out the door. Then I could see this person was a prisoner with cuffs behind his back. The prisoner began running east down the sidewalk. I don't think the deputy even knew the prisoner was escaping as he was still in the process of getting out of the car and gathering up his papers.

I jumped out and started chasing the prisoner. Even with handcuffs, this person was fast. It took me over a block to catch up. From behind, I reached over the person's shoulders, pulling them to the ground. It was then that I realized this person was not a man but a women. She was no more that 5'4", weighing approximately 110 lbs. She presented no problem once she was on the ground. I helped her to her feet and we walked back to the police department.

When I arrived at the booking desk, the deputy was sitting in a small office completing his paperwork and asked if I would book her in. He advised that the woman was picked up from the middle of a busy street in Elk City where she was directing traffic. He also said she was high on PCP.

I shoved the woman against the booking desk with my shoulder which afforded the space I needed to remove her handcuffs. That was a mistake. She wanted to fight, swinging wildly at me while cursing and screaming as loud as possible.

Two (rather large) firemen were standing in the area, in addition to the deputy. The fight was on. She threw one of the men against the wall and kicked another in the chest. After that, we could see she was wearing rather sharp-toed boots with metal decoration. We took the subject to the floor and quickly removed her boots, but in the process, she bit me on the forearm. I put my hand on her throat, choking her until she passed out. All we could think of was that we had to get her in a cell before she came around.

In those days, the city jail was located on the second floor of the building - I have never understood why. We carried her up the steps, then placed her in one of the cells where I was the last to turn loose of her. I placed her on the floor, facing away from the cell door, kicked her feet and legs out from under her, then ran for the door. Other officers were holding the door, ready to slam it as I came out, but in spite of everything, she hit me in the back before I could get out.

I believe she was one of the strongest people I have ever tried to deal with. That is what PCP does to most people.

A few weeks later, my wife and I were shopping in a grocery store in Elk City. As we rounded one of the aisles, who do you suppose we came face-to-face with? You're right; It was the PCP gal. She sort of went into a crouch when she saw me. I told my wife to turn around and we got out of there. I didn't want anymore of that woman.

LYSOL ANYONE?

I think one of the most difficult things to accept as a Probation and Parole Officer, is the devastation of the family unit caused by substance abuse. Whether alcohol or drugs, the family, and especially the children, always suffered. I think alcohol is just as bad, or worse, as illegal drugs. The fact that alcohol was legal, did not make a difference in my mind; It was all bad. If it hurts a child, it is bad.

My partner had one of the worst alcoholics I had ever known. At one time, he had a beautiful family, children, a teaching career and nice home. Alcohol brought him to his knees. Systematically, he lost his family, a member at a time. After they had stepped out of his life, he lost everything; his self-respect, his ability to teach in a public school, his home and future.

One afternoon, we were returning to Elk City from a training session in Oklahoma City. My partner wanted to stop by the man's house to check on him, because of the problems he was having at the time.

We stopped in front of his mobile home, walked up the steps and knocked on the front door. We felt certain he was at home. We continued to knock until it was obvious he was not coming to door, or he was not at home.

We were just starting down the steps when I looked through the living room window. I could see several empty bottles of Lysol on the floor, scattered throughout the front room and kitchen. We knew something was wrong. We began to look closer at the situation. Looking through another window, we finally saw his feet as he lay between the living room and the kitchen. At that point, we kicked the front door in. The man was very close to death. We began trying to revive him, but because of his dire condition, decided to transport him to the hospital.

The man did survive, but only by seconds. If we had not checked on him that day, he would have died.

It's difficult to understand addiction, but when mixed with personal problems, it totally becomes a person's life. Nothing else matters, not family, God, money, love; addiction becomes that person's personal God.

DOGS

When it comes to dogs, Probation and Parole Officers experience some of the same problems as postal workers. When you approach enough houses, you will encounter an unfriendly pooch. I have had my share of encounters, but the only time I was bitten, was by a Chihuahua. It was somewhat embarrassing.

Some of my more industrious clients who dealt in illegal drugs, liked to chain vicious dogs at the front and back of their houses. This type of "get the Probation Officer" mentality often led to their dogs being shot. Although I hated to kill a dog, sometimes it was necessary.

I had a subject in Sayre, who suddenly decided to chain a Doberman at his front door. Having no reason to believe he was a user or dealer of drugs, I walked toward his house one afternoon with no thoughts of a dog. At least, not until I heard a chain being pulled across the wooden porch. I knew what that meant and began to back up. As I had stepped back a couple of steps, I was face to face with a very large, unfriendly dog with very bad breath. I was actually looking down the dog's throat. What I am saying is, we were literally face-to-face. The beast had leaped toward me, mouth open, meaning to take my face off. I had stepped back just in time and barely far enough to avoid a violent contact. The chain stopped the animal in mid air. I felt the dog's hot breath as he was no more than six inches from my face when the chain became taunt. There was no need to draw my weapon. I would probably have dropped it or shot myself in the foot.

By that time, I was so shaken that I returned to my vehicle, called the man on the telephone advising him to come outside and retrieve his animal or I would kill it in his front yard.

It gets much worse. The animal was moved and the owner agreed to get rid of it. We then went into his house where I received another rude awakening. My heart beat was just beginning to return to normal when I saw, coiled up in front of an open flame stove, a Python. It appeared to be full grown, around 15 feet long. To show me it was not dangerous, he slapped it across the head several times . It would hiss and blow, but what else could it do; it was a constrictor. I was less than pleased with the man because the poor choices he had made were now putting his child at risk. The full grown snake could have easily swallowed his young child. I told him the snake had to go or his child had to go. Within the next few days, the man's wife left him taking his daughter.

Problem solved, although I hoped for a different solution.

Canines come in all sizes, but the largest breed I had ever encountered was the St. Bernard. I had always thought they all came with a small keg around their necks. Wrong

I was searching for a client in Elk City one morning, walking around a building, when I heard something. I stopped and listened for a few seconds. If you have ever been to a horse race, then you know what I heard. I was trying to determine the direction the sound was coming from when a St. Bernard rounded the corner - you might say he came around on two paws.   He was about the size of a Volkswagen, running at full speed - whatever that was. There was nothing I could do. It was like being run over by a cement truck. The first part of the dog I encountered was his giant head in the middle of my chest. I actually think he dragged me several feet before I rolled to a stop with no air in my lungs. My glasses were 15 feet away along with a file folder I had been carrying. My white shirt was now a red color matching the soil in Beckham County. And, my tie was hanging down my back rather than in front.

Let me try to better describe this dog/man collision. When I was farming and ranching, I had a rather large Angus bull that contracted the pink eye. Now, Angus cattle are black and rarely have pink eye, but when they do, it is a severe case. This was one of those cases. In fact, the bull was completely blind.

At that time, money was tight.   Pink eye medication was expensive, while plain table salt worked very well as a substitute - and it was inexpensive. The only problem was getting it in the right place. As I was a brilliant "shade-tree veterinarian," I made a decision to simply sneak up on the animal from the front, with salt in each hand. I would casually throw the salt into the bull's eyes and he would fall back. No problem.

My plan, flawed as it was, went off without a hitch, except for one minor issue. When I tossed the salt into the animal's eyes, he did not fall back as I was certain he would. Instead, he came forward. If you have ever had a 1200 pound, blind, mad bull run you down, head first, then you can empathize with me. If you understand what I am talking about, then multiply by two and you will better understand the St. Bernard collision.

I also had a dog in Hollis take the heel off my boot, several years ago.

When I would go into someone's yard, the first thing I looked for was movement of curtains in the house, someone looking out a window, and dog bowls/water dishes in the yard.

This particular day, I saw none of those things as I entered the front gate, and prepared to knock on the front door. I heard the dog coming. It was a Doberman, obviously starved for the past few days in preparation for the Probation Officer's arrival. I almost made it out of the front gate, when the dog grabbed my boot. We did a tug-of-war for a few seconds before he claimed the prize, which was the heel of my boot. I simply declared him the winner and left. I would later order the client to rid himself of the "leather loving" dog.

Just one more canine story before I move along. I have a good friend who was the Undersheriff in Greer County, several years ago. He was also the canine officer, and a good one.

His police dog came from Germany and had the biggest head of any dog I had ever seen. They may have breed them that way so they would have more teeth, but probably not. He was an excellent police canine although he had the head of a horse.

One day I was going into the sheriff's office, for some reason. The front door is glass, affording anyone inside to see who is coming or going, however, the reflective material restricted the vision of the person coming from the outside. The dog was standing at the door looking out when I jerked the door open. That has always been one of my bad habits. I don't just open a door, I jerk it open.

True to form, I jerked the front door open with my left hand as the dog grabbed my right hand. We both just stared at each other. I was certainly not going to move and lose a hand. He simply held me, not loose and not overly tight. A simple command from his handler and he turned loose, sat down and seemed to smile at me. It was not funny, but I never jerked the door open again.

THE MENTALLY ILL

I could easily fill a book with the mentally disturbed individuals I have contacted through the years. I have seen people with tinfoil over their windows, tinfoil over everything in the house, with hopes of keeping the authorities from spying on them. While others might hallucinate or imagine things that were not possible. I remember answering a call once where the individual said the electricity was running out of the outlet into the floor. The person could actually see it. I was always sad to see people battling for their sanity while dealing with other serious problems.

There was a man in Greer County who experienced these type of problems, to the point that he required hospitalization from time to time. Although on medication, when he began to feel better, he would discontinue its use, something common with people suffering from these conditions.

I was asked one day, to assist in going to his home where he would be taken into protective custody. He was, again, off his medication. I reluctantly agreed to help. I am talking about a man who was married, had a family and was extremely dangerous when off his medication. To make matters worse, he was probably the strongest man I have ever known. I recalled the times when he and his family hauled hay for us. Our peanut hay was very light, which presented no problems. Alfalfa, however, was extremely heavy. It took a strong man to handle that type of hay when it was green.

This man could throw a bale of alfalfa completely over a mostly-loaded truck. It was almost unbelievable.

We "gathered the troops" and drove out to his place. His house was located about a quarter-mile off the main road in the north part of the county near Lake Creek. As we pulled off the main road and drove toward his house, we heard gunshots. We stopped, got out of the patrol units for a better view, then we could see the man standing in his front yard firing at us with a shotgun. We could see where the shotgun pellets were striking the ground more that a hundred yards in front of our vehicles. It was apparent he was using birdshot in the weapon. The sheriff had advised his dispatcher of the situation and of our safety. We knew people in the area would be calling in, reporting the gunshots.

It was about that time that an FBI Agent, who worked the area, slid to a stop in the main road. He became excited when another shot was fired in our direction. He made the comment, "I'll stop this crap." He popped the trunk lid on his vehicle, removed a 30-06 rifle with a mounted scope, placed it across the hood of the car, then began the process of sighting in. We began to explain the situation and the fact that the man was mentally ill and off his medication. Once he heard the explanation, he placed the rifle back in his car.

We continued to observe the subject in his front yard. He walked back and forth for a few minutes, fired a few more shots, then sat the gun down against the side of the house. He then walked over to his Oldsmobile vehicle, grabbed the front bumper, picking it off the ground. I'm talking about the front end of a heavy vehicle. But that wasn't the end of it. He then took a couple of steps before dropping it. It bounced a couple of times before he disappeared into his house. Several thoughts ran through my mind. This man could easily throw me through any wall in his house. In fact, he was capable of throwing any of us through the house. Not a comforting thought. Before long, he was asleep and was taken into custody without further incident.

A very sad situation, especially for his family. When he was on his medication, he seemed to be a normal person. When he was not, he was a superman and a bad guy.

A BAD DAY

We have all experienced bad days, but some worse than others. This was starting out to be a bad day.

I recall a black man on probation in Mangum who was continually having problems with employment, family and finances. It worried him that he was unable to pay his bills or take care of his family.

One day, his wife came to my office advising he had run her and the children out of the house. He barricaded himself in the house and was in the process of taking all the inside and closet doors off their hinges. He was then nailing them over the windows inside the house. She didn't know if he had weapons other than several knives. She had no idea what his problem was, but was afraid of him.

I took a couple police officers with me, first attempting to contact the man by telephone. We then called to him on a bull horn, but no response. We waited for several hours while trying to make contact, but nothing seemed to work.

Knowing the man fairly well, I finally put on a ballistic vest, walked up to his house and knocked on the door. To my surprise, he opened the front door. I asked him to step out of the house and place his hands on the wall, which he did. After I searched him for weapons, I asked him what was going on. I'll never forget his answer; "I'm just having a bad day."

Well, that was certainly an under-statement! Do you take all the inside doors off their hinges and nail them over the windows when your day doesn't go just right? I thought not - neither do I.

He was taken to the police department where I spent some time talking with him. When it was determined that he was not a risk to himself, his family or others, he was released with the promise he would enter a treatment program to deal with his extreme anxiety.

End of story......until next time.

THE WHITE BULLDOG

I was ordered to conduct a pre-sentence investigation on a man who had killed his father in Custer County. I don't remember the circumstances involved in the case, except that he told authorities his white bulldog told him to kill his father.

During my investigation, I sat down with the individual at the Custer County Jail. He answered questions as I made inquiries, looked me in the eye and just, generally, seemed to understand the situation. However, during my interview, he suddenly jumped almost out of his seat, dodging to one side as if someone had thrown something at him. I ignored the first such occurrence, but on the second, asked him about it. He said, "Didn't you see that?" My answer, of course, was no. This continued to go on for the next 30 minutes.

On about the tenth episode, I asked again. This time, he said, "The spot, the yellow spot, don't you see it? It's right up there on the wall." I asked him about the spot. "It's about this big (his arms made a circle of approximately 2' around) and it changes shapes. It's bright yellow. Don't you see it?" Of course I did not, but he could. I could see his eyes focus on something when he looked in that direction. He was certainly seeing it.

During the latter part of the investigation, I contacted the defendant's mother. I remember walking up to her front door where I was greeted by her son's white bulldog. Yes, I thought about it, but no, I did not ask any questions. Like the rest of us, he probably didn't know the answers anyway.

THE SCUM OF THE EARTH

If this heading offends you, I will apologize now. But there are two categories of offenders that deserve this label: those who prey on children and those who take advantage of the elderly. I have little sympathy for them, always taking every opportunity to take them off the streets.

One such offender was taking advantage of the elderly and

those who lived alone, in the Mangum area. He called himself a handyman, claiming all types of skills, excellent workmanship, general knowledge of plants, but was a fraud, interested only in himself. For some time, I knew what he was doing, but none of his victims were willing to fill out a complaint on him; they were afraid of him. He was a tall black man, talked very loud and simply had a demanding appearance, which he used to his advantage. He would go to an elderly woman's home, demand to do work for her, then move a few leaves around - most of the time he did nothing - then demand a large payment for his labor. Most people, but especially the older women who lived alone, simply paid him what he asked without looking at his work. They were afraid of him; he made sure of that.

I talked with several of the elderly women, but they were not willing to point the finger at him. The older men were the same; they did not want to cause any problems for him. Simply put, this conman knew what he was doing in putting fear in these people.

I had a good friend who lived next to one of the victims. Peggy and George Roach checked on the man and took him food. He was an elderly gentleman, lived alone with only limited income. He could barely exist on his meager income. I knew my client had been at his house on occasion, but had no proof that he had cheated the old man. I asked the neighbor to call if she saw the man around.

One afternoon, I received a call from Peggy, telling me the man I was investigating had just walked into her neighbor's home, without knocking. When I arrived, I walked into house, catching my client red-handed. He was standing over the elderly man telling him how much to make the check for. I can't recall the exact amount, but I do know it was exorbitant. I asked the subject to show me what work he had done. We left the house walking to the rear of the property where he said he had been working. Although he claimed to have raked some leaves, I saw nothing he had done. He stammered and struggled to find some type of work he had performed, but could not.

I placed him under arrest and placed restraints on him. He began to argue and failed to comply with my orders. As he argued or stop walking toward my car, I would have to push him. He was taken to the Greer County Jail.

I received permission from the victim to search through his checking account and bank records. What I found was extremely disturbing to me. My probationer had been doing the same thing for several months, collecting hundreds of dollars from this kind old gentleman while doing little or no work for him.

Fraud charges were filed along with probation revocation on a former offense. At the Greer County jail, while I was interviewing him, he told me he just needed some help with his problems. I assured him I would get him some help, about 20 years worth. He said he didn't need quite that much help.

I don't remember the exact sentence, but it wasn't long enough. The moral of the story was; "Don't ask for help if you're not ready for it."

KEEP YOUR WEAPON CLEAN

I had just pulled into a parking space at the Beckham County Sheriff's Department when a deputy came running out and said, "Lets go!."

The next thing I knew, we were at an apartment complex south of the Courthouse in Sayre. The Sheriff was standing in front of an open door at one of the apartments holding a small board. In the doorway of the apartment was an individual holding a butcher knife in each hand. The deputy and I both drew our weapons and trained them on the person in the doorway while the Sheriff continued trying to talk with him. It was obvious the man was not in his right mind, however, the Sheriff was standing much too close to the knives. I was not sure I could fire quick enough if he lunged forward.

Suddenly, the man threw one of the knives down, turned and ran down a hallway in the apartment. The Sheriff handed me his service revolver, entered the apartment with only a small 1" x 4 " board, chasing the man through the apartment. I slipped the revolver in the small of my back before entering the apartment. The deputy and I cornered the person inside the apartment where he surrendered at gunpoint.

Once we had the individual at the sheriff's office, I was going to return the Sheriff's revolver, that is, until I looked at it. The front of the cylinder was green with corrosion. When I attempted the open the cylinder, it would not budge. I finally used a small section of a 2 x 4 against the cylinder, while striking it with a hammer. It took several blows before the weapon opened. I had never seen a weapon in that kind of condition. The bullets had obviously been in the weapon for years. I used a brass rod and hammer to remove the bullets from the cylinder. The primers were corroded to the point that they would certainly not have fired. The Model 66 Smith and Wesson Pistol was ruined. The cylinder was so pitted, as was much of the weapon, that it would not have been safe to fire it. I cleaned it the best I could and returned it to the sheriff. I told him it would not be safe to fire, to which he said, "That's alright, I never shoot it anyway."

Your tax dollars at work.

DEAD CHICKENS

You can ask anyone and they will verify that I do not like chickens. I eat fowl only if there is nothing else available, or my wife tells me to eat it. I have never been a serious conesuier of poultry. Just for your information, chicken is not classified as meat; It is fowl.

My sense of smell has always been very poor; I suppose I inherited the olfactory disability from my Father who could lay down and sleep with a skunk.

This would be a day to test my fortitude as well as my sense of smell. I was at the Sheriff's Office in Sayre one morning when I was asked to take a call in the northwest area of the county. They had no deputies available to take the call, at that time. I agree, then headed toward Sweetwater. The call received by the Sheriff's Office was made from a convenience store in Sweetwater. The report involved an elderly man who appeared to be disoriented and lost.

When I arrived at the store and walked inside, I was met by the owner who pointed out the person he had called about. He was sitting on a stool near the front counter. The man was around 75 years old, decently dressed and friendly. I sat down with him, advised of my identity then asked where he had come from and where he was going.

"I'm on my way to Kansas City to see an old friend of mine," he said. When I asked him where he had come from, his answer was somewhat illusive, but it was the Oklahoma City area.

I ran the registration on his vehicle after taking his keys. The car checked to his son in Oklahoma City. When I called his son, explaining the situation, he was relieved. He told me his father had left from a nursing home in Oklahoma City after "borrowing" his vehicle. He asked that we hold his father until he could come and get him. I agreed.

When I opened the door of the old man's car, the stench almost knocked me over. Looking the rear of the vehicle, I found approximately 10 dead chickens. When I say they were dead, I mean they had been dead for several days. I asked the old gentleman about the dead chickens. He said, "I traded a guy on the road my rods and reels for the chickens. I plan to eat them later."

We held the old man at the Beckham County Sheriff's Department until his son made arraingments to come and get him.

My sense of smell had been tested to the limits that day; my feelings about chickens were only reinforced.

It was good to actually help someone, for a change.

UNPOPULAR ARRESTS

I suppose any time someone in taken into custody, there are those who are very unhappy. I have witnessed some of them, up close. Some of the law enforcement officers in Beckham County, jokingly said they were going to stop going to lunch with me because I often arrested someone.

One day, I was with several officers having lunch at a resturant in Sayre. There was the normal conversation; who's selling drugs out of their house, who do you think is the burglar hitting the country barns, have you seen this guy or that guy. It was just another day.

There was a man eating alone several tables away from us who would occasionally look at me, but I did not recognize him. He had a full beard, his hair was unkempt, just a normal individual. But the more I looked at him, the more he reminded me of someone. I just couldn't come up with a name. About the time I had finished eating, the name came to me. I had not seen the man in several months.

I walked over to the house phone, called the police department asking the dispatcher to verify an outstanding Oklahoma Department of Corrections Parole Warrant on the individual. The warrant was still outstanding.

I walked toward the man's table and was almost there when he threw his fork across the table. He said, "Hell yes it's me; I didn't think you would recognize me, but it didn't work out." I encouraged him to finish eating, but he said, "I've lost my appetite."

What I didn't know was the man was driving a double-decker, 18-wheeler, loaded with cattle. We had to impound the truck and it's contents when I placed the man under arrest. We also had to "lot" the cattle with the local livestock yard where they were held until the owner could make arrangement to come to Sayre.

I was not a very popular person for a while, but you can't allow a felon to walk off, or so my first supervisor explained to me. I could always eat alone.

PRACTICAL JOKES

In this case, I think we could say, "Impractical" jokes. We have all seen practical jokes carried to the extreme, but this was by far, the most extreme I have witnessed.

Police officers, or peace officers in general, are notorious for pulling pranks on each other. Working with so many different law enforcement agencies and departments, I witnessed some strange activities.

With the introduction of pepper spray to officers, new and more adventurous avenues were available for jokers. They would spray the chemical on another officer's steering wheel, under the door handles, or as I witnessed once, put a can of pepper spray under a vehicle seat, setting it up far enough that any pressure on the seat would activate the spray. Believe me, it will fill a vehicle in seconds, and you will not be able to get a breath.

There was a particular officer with the Mangum Police Department who took practical jokes to the limit. It was a little scary to work around him, not knowing what he was planning next. Whether it was a "For Sale" sign in the yard, an ad in the local newspaper, or something more sinister, he lived for practical jokes.

As the pranks bounced back and forth between that officer and other staff, things seemed to be getting more and more extreme, until one day when I overheard other officers discussing a way to "get him good." I couldn't believe what they were planning. Since the officer and his family were out of town on vacation, they were plotting to move his house. It was not a small house, it was a large house sitting on a major street in Mangum. It was frightening, but luckily, never materialized. That's what I would call a real "Impractical" joke.

YOU HAVE HOW MANY CHILDREN?

That was the question the Oklahoma Department of Human Services ask when I called them.

I was sitting in the Mangum Office, minding my own business, when a woman walked through my door. She said she was told by a Probation and Parole Officer in another district to report to my office upon her arrival in Mangum. Because she acted very nervous and constantly glanced out the window, I ran a record check on her and found an outstanding felony warrant from another county. I advised her of the warrant, which she apparently knew about. She asked about options.

I knew nothing of this woman - no file, no background, family, nothing. I placed the woman under arrest and she began to cry, which was not unusual, as many women placed under arrest become very emotional. What she then explained to me, caused me to become emotional. She had six children outside in her vehicle, one of which was a paraplegic. I immediately called the county from which the warrant was issued, asking them if she couldn't simply come in or her own. They advised, "Under no circumstances was I to release her." They had been trying to find her for months.

When I called Human Services in Greer County, I could hear the gasps and whispers. They said they did not have facilities lined up to handle that many children, especially the one with physical problems. I told them they had no choice.

When they came to get the children, I was the recipient of numerous "go-to-hell" looks. I think some of workers still hate me today, and I can't really blame them. Sometimes, it was a dirty job.

TOMATOS AND MARIJUANA

I have seen marijuana growing about everywhere; ditches, inside of cars, basements, on rooftops, near farm ponds, back porches, patios, caves and in plain sight, but this was a first.

I was searching for a young black man who had only recently established residence with his grandmother in Mangum. I talked with the woman for a few minutes - just small talk. Her grandson should be home by dark, she said.

As I left the woman's residence, walking back to my car, I was admiring her beautiful garden: tomatoes, beans, cantaloupes, okra, beets. It was a beautiful garden.

I was almost to my vehicle, when I noticed something strange about the tomato plants. The tops of the vines were somewhat ragged. I walked to the garden, finding marijuana plants growing between each tomato plant. I think there were about four rows of tomato plants with large marijuana plants between each garden plant.

I telephoned the county sheriff and police department advising what I had found. When other officers arrived, we began pulling the plants out of the ground, putting them in the trunk of one of the units. I went back to the woman's house and began talking with her.

This was close to our conversation.

"Did you know there were marijuana plants in your garden?"

"Yes sir"

"Do you think your grandson may have put them there?"

"No sir"

"What do you mean?"

"I mean, I put them there."

"Are you telling me you planted the marijuana?"

"Yes sir"

"Could you tell me your age?"

"I'm 85 years old"

"Do you have anymore in your house?"

"Yes sir, thay's some under my bed."

The woman invited me into the house where I found two large aluminum pans heaped with drying marijuana under her bed. I added this to the collection taken from the garden.

"What were you doing with all this?"

"I wuz selling it - hard to make a living around here. What you gonna do with a 85 year old woman?" She had a good point.

I talked with the sheriff and police chief about the situation. I did not want to arrest the woman, but neither did either of them. We simply bid her farewell with a warning not to grow anymore marijuana, loaded up the contraband, and left.

Sometimes you win, sometimes you just get the "dope".

THE JUNKMAN OR DUMB CROOK FILE

This guy was a real character. I always called him "the junkman" because he never stole anything of real value, that I was aware of. I can't even remember how he managed to be on probation, with his aversion to nice things. If there was ever a burglary of things that would not work, or if only junk was taken, I went to see this man.

A burglary and the larceny of a vehicle occurred one night south of Sayre. Along with those crimes, the suspect had crashed through a gate, tore the camper shell off the truck and stole some items of very little value. I was in the sheriff's office the next morning reading through reports when I came across this one. It had to be my "junkman."

The truck had been recovered - in the median of Interstate 40 - only a couple of miles from town. The battery had been removed, but the suspect left a rather large tennis shoe in the pickup bed.

There was little need to look any further. I drove directly to his house. As I stopped in his driveway, I could see an old junked car near the house, with a new battery in it - this vehicle had no wheels. Don't ask. I don't have a clue.

When I knocked, he opened the door and immediately looked down. Inside the living room was the stolen property, stacked in a corner. It was not funny, however, I think I let out a small chuckle. The items stolen were stacked in the same order as they were listed in the sheriff's report. He didn't remember why he left his shoe, but readily admitted to the crimes. Apparently, he carried the battery over two miles while wearing only 1 shoe.

I made him load the items in the trunk of my car, then we went to jail - again. This was a pitiful case and one I didn't enjoy being involved in.

REALLY DUMB CROOK

Some people's thought patterns simply work differently than others. In this case, I would say the reasoning was somewhat off.

I had a probationer who operated a small tire shop. He sold tires, tubes, rims and automobile accessories. He came in one day to advise that someone had broken into his shop the night before, taking only a set of polished, chrome rims. A police report was taken.

I believe it was the next day that I was making a home visit on a probationer who lived within 50 yards of the tire shop. As I walked up the driveway, I noticed the new chrome rims on his vehicle and asked him about them. It was obvious from his expression that something was wrong. When I asked him where he had bought the new rims, he simply could not lie and admitted breaking into the tire shop. I arrested him then placed him in the Greer County Jail. The rims were recovered and everyone was happy, with the exception of my newest dumb crook. There is one thing I can compliment this man for; his honesty in admitting to the theft.

I suppose that case was no worse than a man reporting to my office in Elk City with a baggie of marijuana in his shirt pocket, then telling me it belonged to his roommate. Brilliant.

There are individuals who simply cannot help self-destruction. But I must admit, I have always felt a ting of shame for my actions in dealing with a rather "slow" crook. I made preparation for his arrival at my office, knowing he had committed a burglary, and also knowing I had no evidence of the crime.

Before he came in, I printed the word "lie" on a regular sheet of copy paper and placed it in my copy machine. I also ran a couple of colored speaker wires from the back of the copier and placed strips of Velcro at the end of each wire.

After visiting with the young man for a few minutes, he denied any knowledge of the burglary. I asked if he would take a polygraph exam, to which he agreed. I placed the Velcro on his wrists and began to question him. When I was sure he was lying, I would activate the copier and show him the word "lie." After a few minutes (and a few falsehoods) he admitted to the crime. My polygraph/copier had lived up to my expectations. I almost felt sorry for him. Who said life was fair.

A CLOSE CALL

I knew when I started this job, it could be dangerous. I tried not to think about it, knowing my wife worried enough for both of us. A few years prior to the incident I am about to describe, I had turned in a state vehicle with a bullet hole above the windshield, however, the shooter was never positively identified.

But this was a day I almost became a statistic; It was a close call.

I had gone into the Strong City area in Roger Mills County to make contact with one of my probationers. He lived several miles from Cheyenne, which was the county seat. It would be just a routine visit - I would later learn no home visit was routine.

When I arrived at the house, I walked up to the door and knocked. A voice on the other side invited me in. I walked in. My client was sitting on a couch, no shirt or shoes but with a handgun holster between his feet. I could also see numerous packages around the room which appeared to be illegal drugs. There was no weapon in sight. As I asked if he had a weapon, he took off through an archway toward an open bedroom. He stopped in front of a bed, still with his back to me, and was looking down at something.

I had warned him to stop, however I could tell he was trying to retrieve something from the bed. I had to assume it was a weapon. As I waited for him to turn around, I placed the front sight of my revolver in the middle of his back, hoping he would give up. I remember thinking this was going to be mess, with white stucco walls in the bedroom and the hollow-point magnum ammunition I was using. He gave up.

I backed him out of the house, took him out into the yard and handcuffed him to an old car sitting in the yard. I then returned to the house, performed a quick search for anyone who might have been in the home, and picked up the weapons from the bed. What I had not seen was the Luger Semi-automatic Pistol under a red flannel shirt on the bed, and a sawed-off, 20-gauge shotgun at the end of the bed. Both were loaded.

I locked the house, loaded my prisoner and headed for Cheyenne. On the way, I attempted to alert someone by radio. I finally raised a deputy who was on his way to my location.

After only a few miles, I met the Roger Mills County deputy who had stopped. He saw who I had in the car and said, "I was just on my way to his house with a search warrant." That remark certainly didn't slow my heart rate. It was still pounding inside my chest like a trip-hammer. It would continue at that pace for the remainder of the day.

Once I arrived at Cheyenne and placed my prisoner in jail, I went back to the location with the deputy. We recovered enough packaged narcotics to almost fill the trunk of his car. He also had them arranged by drug with price tags on most of them. It was easy to see what he had been doing.

I took a hard look at my job. My wife wanted me to quit, which, I must say, I almost did. For the next several weeks, I would weigh my job against the dangers involved.

In a few days, I was back in Cheyenne visiting in the sheriff's office. One of the jail staff gave me a small drawing made by the man I brought in. It was a crude drawing of a man shooting an officer with a shotgun. I wonder what he had in mind that day.

The hard lessons we learn are usually the most important ones. I learned that day, the importance of good, constant communication with law enforcement agencies in the areas where you work. I would not forget that valuable lesson, especially after it almost cost me my life.

As I would train officers in the future, that was one of the most important aspects of the job I tried to get across to them. Know the law enforcement officers in the counties you work. They know your people, where they live, what they are doing, who they associate with and their families. Stay close to them; they are your main source of information and your only backup in the field, especially in rural areas.

THE OIL BOOM

In the late 1970s and early 1980s, the red dirt of Beckam County saw an extreme change. Oil and gas exploration suddenly turned from searching, to deep well drilling. Prices for petroleum products were up and the boom was on, and was it a boom. The Anadarko Basin began to yield record volumes of natural gas and oil. It was predicted to last for 20 years as more and countless individuals staked their hopes, dreams, and money on what it was to become.

Almost overnight, metal buildings sprang up everywhere, oil

and gas drilling derricks were as plentiful as windmills and mailboxes across the rolling hills. Oil companies and subsidiary businesses followed the derricks into town by the hundreds, with drilling equipment that could only be measured by the tonnage. It was an overnight facelift for Western Oklahoma which brought instant wealth for some, and heartaches for others.

Of course, the Anadarko Basin covered more area that just Beckham County, but for a Probation and Parole Officer who worked primarily alone, it had set up in my backyard - Elk City. It was no longer a sleepy little town with its down-home, home-town atmosphere of boots and hats, "Howdy Ma'm," hay bales and pickups; it was a different crowd.

Oil field workers flooded the area, drawn by high wages and more than enough work to go around. A man could quit his job one day, walk across the road and get another for more money, because he had experience. It was hard, dangerous work but good money, which brought in all types - some good, some bad. The bad, I would become acquainted with, the good I wouldn't know.

But, where there is money, there is crime, and we had plenty of both. At the peak of the boom, I was averaging one new client each day, drawn to the area for the work and high pay. I remember talking with one man from Michigan, who told me there was a billboard in his hometown pointing workers to Elk City, Oklahoma, to the oil fields, long term employment and easy money.

Housing was in short supply. People lived in tents, under trees, under bridges, in their cars and abandoned farm houses in the country. I regularly had coffee with a man who lived in his car. I don't know how he did it.

I also had a client who was lived in a cellar, and although it had a dirt floor, it was one of the cleaner places I had seen. If you think it difficult to locate someone, try finding them in a tent city. We had one for some time in Elk City.

For me, it was overwhelming. The new population was a different breed; they worked hard, but they played harder. The crime rate began to climb along with my caseload as barroom brawls and shootings were the norm. I stopped running tag numbers; I didn't have time to deal with stolen vehicles, their drivers and paperwork. It was all I could do to keep up with the normal paperwork required by the department, reports for the courts, violation reports and case openings. The department said they were trying to get the help I needed, but by then, I would be into my second or third year.

For month after month, I got up in the morning with a knot in my stomach, then came home at night in the same, or worse, condition.

As a Probation and Parole Officer in a rural area of Oklahoma and during the oil boom, the on-call time was 24/7. There were telephone calls in the middle of the night, many of which required immediate action; if you turned your pager and cell phone off, you were in violation of policy, but even if you did, the police would be knocking on your door to advise you to call here or there. It was a difficult job during those years, even though I did eventually have other officers working with me. The department almost waited too long.

Elk City began to see faction gangs battling for drug distribution rights in the area, closely followed by a dramatic increase in homicides. Each group was suspected of having its own enforcer. At last count, I think there are still eight unsolved homicides in the county, all of which were directly related to the influx of gang members and their trade. The area between Carter and Elk City turned into a dumping ground for murder victims.

Every firearm I confiscated, was test fired and the casing sent to the State Bureau of Investigation for ballistic comparison tests.

During the height of the boom, I was experiencing problems with a particular parolee. He was constantly in bars, fighting and keeping company with other felons. I was monitoring him very closely due to numerous rule violations and suspected criminal ties with a motorcycle gang who called themselves the Outlaws. They had moved in with the high paying jobs and big money. One night, he left a bar on his motorcycle on his way home, when he had a head-on collision with a Mack Truck. There was very little left of the motorcycle or its rider.

The gang felt I was partly responsible for the accident because of my supervision methods. They began to intimidate me. I would be at someone's home or talking with them in their yard when a couple of gang members on motorcycles would stop in front and just stare at me. Occasionally, one would point his finger at me, mimicking a pistol's falling hammer. This was about the time I began to carry two handguns, and a switchblade knife.

They often followed me around town in an effort to scare or intimidate me. After a few weeks, it all stopped. I never knew why. Perhaps they found someone more deserving of their attention.

CONVICT OR I'LL JUMP

I know it's a strange title, but the story is somewhat strange. It was not unusual for an officer to confiscate weapons in Elk City during the boom. I had a female probationer who operated a motel and who was caught with a sawed-off shotgun in her possession. Actually, she kept it at the desk in the motel, but it was a felony to have such a weapon, and a violation of her probation.

Woodward County filed a motion to revoke her probation soon after receiving a violation report from this officer. The assistant district attorney requested that I bring the weapon as evidence in the case.

On the day of the hearing, I entered the courthouse with the sawed-off shotgun wrapped in an old rain coat. It was given to the prosecution as evidence and the hearing began. The young assistant was about as flamboyant or audacious a prosecutor as I had ever been around. He didn't just unwrap the weapon, he jerked the end of the jacket, allowing the gun to bounce around on the state's table. It did have an effect.

As he rested the state's case, he made the comment that he would jump out the courtroom window if the court chose not to revoke (this would have been from the second or third story). Luckily for all of us, and especially the assistant district attorney, the person's probation was revoked.

Barnum and Bailey would have been proud.

LET'S SCARE THE PAROLE OFFICER

I had gone to an apartment in Elk City to locate, interview and open a case on a transfer from another state. As the case with many oil field workers, housing was in short supply and several men would often share an apartment. That was the case on this day.

I was looking at nine men in this particular apartment. The person I was interviewing was pleasant enough. I had positioned myself with my back against the wall and where I could see most of the other individuals. As I was writing, I suddenly heard the sound of a revolver cylinder spin. It was a very distinctive sound which brought chill bumps and adrenalin. As I stood, with my hand on my weapon, I watched one of the men toss a rather large .44 caliber revolver on the floor.

The individual I was interviewing began to apologize for his friend. I marched them all outside after picking up the weapon and began running record checks on all of them. Although most of them were apologizing by now, it would cost one of them his freedom. The individual who spun the cylinder on the pistol, said; "We were just having a little fun and scaring the parole officer."

They succeeded in scaring me, but one of the men was wanted on a warrant out of Ohio. He went to jail. "Scaring the Parole Officer wasn't all that funny," one of them said.

I learned a lesson that day that has followed me, even into retirement. I always sit with my back to the wall. I know this sometimes bothers my wife when we go out to eat, but like some other habits I developed during the oil boom, it stemmed from incidents as I just described.

We all develop habits during our lives, some of which will follow us to our graves. Another of mine is tapping of the side of the mailbox before I open the lid. Years ago, a probationer put a diamond-backed rattlesnake in an officer's mailbox. Luckily, it alerted him as he approached, and he was not bitten. That has stuck with me all these years. Yea, I know, but I just can't stop doing it.

DON'T CARRY YOUR WEAPON IN YOUR BOOT

I know this sounds strange, but allow me to elaborate. I had an office in Mangum at the time. Having always worked closely with the Oklahoma State Reformatory as well as local law enforcement, I often assisted them when they requested help.

I received a call one day from the Chief of Security advising one of the cooks from the prison had left the grounds. He was thought to be in the Mangum area. They gave me a family name in the area thinking he could be with some of them.

I was into western wear at the time, usually wearing boots, colored jeans, a knit shirt and a blazer. When the weather was too warm for a jacket, I carried my .38 caliber revolver in my right boot.

I knocked on several doors, ran some tags and talked with several people about the escapee, but received little quality information. The next door I knocked on was an eye-opener. The escapee answered the door, still in his white, kitchen clothing. He waited patiently while I dug my weapon out of my boot and took him into custody. If he had been armed, he would have shot me in the top of the head.

Don't carry your primary weapon in your boot, for crying out loud.

THE WARDEN'S HOUSEBOY

Another call. The State Reformatory Warden, this time. It seems his houseboy left the area with his girlfriend, whom I had the misfortune of knowing. She was from Mangum.

I drove to the facility where I picked up my brother, who was the facility training officer at the time. We drove directly to the girlfriend's house, but she was in the process of leaving. The man was not in her vehicle and she denied any knowledge of his whereabouts. She also denied picking him up at the prison just a few minutes before, which we knew to be a lie.

Knowing we could pick her up anytime, we allowed her to leave. When she was out of sight, we checked the house, finding the front door screen latched from the inside. Now, how did that happen? She just said there was no one in her house. We called the sheriff's office and requested additional support, because, and according to my brother, the warden's houseboy was a black man about the size of a large refrigerator. Great, just great.

It was only a few minutes until a couple of officers arrived. We knocked on the front and back doors, but received no response. We discussed a course of action, settling on breaking into the house through one of the back windows. We felt we had sufficient probable cause, due to the circumstances. We felt certain the escapee was inside since we had observed his girlfriend leave the house through the front door. Someone had to be inside.

We found a window unlocked at the rear of the residence, allowing us to gain entry without damaging any of the exterior. Once inside, we began a search for the man. It was only a few minutes before we found him in a closet, standing very erect, arms held tightly against his sides, with his eyes shut. He was taken into custody without incident, other than, perhaps a chuckle or two.

As David and I returned the inmate to the State Reformatory and as we walked up the front walkway toward the main entrance, the inmate had one request. "Mr. Morris, would you please take these handcuffs off? The warden is going to be mad as hell. I'd like to be able to protect myself."

His request, of course, was denied. He was charged with Escape From a Penal Institution and his girlfriend with Aiding and Abetting an Escape.

Our actions sometimes produce undesirable consequences.

MAN WITH KNIFE

I don't like knives. From the time I was a small child, I have had a fear of being stabbed or cut, so much so, that it caused me great concern over the years. I always said I had rather be shot than stabbed, although the survival rate would be greater with a knife wound.

I contacted a young man in Elk City who lived alone in a mobile home. He was always compliant with an interest in making a change in his life. I walked up the three or four steps to the front door and knocked. There was barely enough room on the step for the front door to open because of the small porch and rail.

I tried to listen for movement inside when, suddenly, the front door opened. All I focused on was the knife the man had in his upraised hand. I did notice that he had blood on his face. I always carried a small, leather folder with various forms and notations of the clients I was attempting to contact. When I saw him holding the knife (positioned over his head), I pitched the folder at the man's face in a frisbee-toss motion, at the same time, I drew my weapon. Just before I pulled the trigger, I heard him saying "No, No, I didn't know it was you! I thought you were him coming back!" That had little bearing on the situation I was facing. The only thing that saved him was that he dropped the knife and stepping back inside the trailer.

After both of us regained some composure, he told me a friend of his had been with him a few minutes before I came. They were arguing about something which led to a physical altercation. During the incident, his friend (using the term loosely) used a church-key on his face. There was a 10" to 12" cut across his face, similar to what such a device would have accomplished. He also had blood on his face an shirt. I didn't have to warn him about his actions; he knew his impulsive behavior almost caused his death. He was still apologizing as I left. Another near heart attack.

As I said, I hate knives for the damage they are capable of doing. I actually carried a switch-blade for two or three years during the oil boom. I usually taped it to my leg just above my shoe, or sometimes, carried it in my back pocket. Fortunately, I never had to use it.

STOLEN FIREARMS

In my opinion, one of the most serious violations of parole has to be the possession of a firearm. During the oil boom, I suspected one of my parolees broke into a gun shop in Elk City and took dozens of firearms. I received information indicating he was selling the weapons to various people in the Clinton and Weatherford area.

An Elk City Detective and I, along with two officers from Clinton, attempted to set up a sting in which we hoped to buy one of the weapons. We rented a motel room in Weatherford where the parolee was living at the time. We had an informant who agreed to contact him by phone and purchase one of the weapons.

It was late at night when our informant was able to contact the parolee. He agreed to leave the weapon at a certain location outside of town and requested the money be left at that place. We did not attempt to watch the exchange as we feared he would sense problems and possibly injure the informant.

Everything worked as planned. The exchange was made and the weapon brought back to the motel. We verified the weapon was stolen from the gun shop and waited until morning to request a warrant for his arrest.

In the morning, I attempted to locate the parolee as I could pick him up on an emergency department warrant. The Elk City Detective and I went to the college campus in Weatherford where it was reported he lived with his girlfriend. We knew he was in the trailer park when we spotted his vehicle in the parking lot. I took a pair of pliers and pulled the valve stems out of his tires, in case he decided to run.

Over an hour later we located the girl's trailer where he was reportedly living. The detective covered the back door as I knocked on the front. It had been reported to us that the man was carrying a pistol. I had my weapon at my side while at the door. I think both of us were surprised when he answered the door. I held him at gunpoint and shouted to my friend at the back. We searched him for weapons, restrained him and transported him to the county jail.

I was happy to get home that morning, although I had to return to work in a few hours. The weapons were located and charges filed against my client, in addition to revocation of his parole and the remainder of his prison term.

Some things work out, at times.

PRECIOUS CHILD

I have never understood, nor had any sympathy for parents who failed to properly care for their children. There is nothing in this life more pure or holy than a little child. Jesus said that each of us would be required to become as a little child before we would be worthy of the Kingdom of Heaven.

During my years as an officer, I have seen child abuse beyond description. I have taken children from homes where a normal person wouldn't have an animal living. To witness that level of abuse has always broken my heart.

I was driving down Seventh Street in Elk City when I saw a baby standing in the middle of the street. Even though the weather was cold that morning, the child wore only a diaper. The little girl who was no more that a year old, was crying and freezing. I wrapped the child in my jacket, then took her to the police department where a female officer cared for her while the Chief and I searched for the parents.

We were more than an hour locating the person responsible for the child - the father (I use the term loosely). I found the Mexican man sitting in his backyard whittling on a piece of wood. After I described the baby, I asked if there was a child in the house. He said his baby was in the house asleep, so the lost child could not be his. I asked him to check to make sure. Sure enough, his child was gone. He seemed unconcerned when I told him the baby was picked up in the middle of the street about a block from his house. He still seemed unconcerned as he told us he would come to the police department and retrieve the baby. I told him to stop what he was doing and look at me. As he tried to face me (which he could not do) I assured him if he came to the police department, I would put him in jail. I explained his pathetic parenting skills while telling him he didn't deserve a child. I then left before I punched him in the nose.

The man was referred to the Department of Human Services as they would have the child, along with a request for a full investigation. The Chief and I had to get away from the man before one of us lost control.

Although I have taken other children from homes as they were deemed "in danger," the most memorable was a little girl about a year old. She was a beautiful child with blond hair and a smile that would melt ice.

I was searching for a couple who had only recently transferred their probation supervision from Arkansas. I knew they were living in a small travel trailer, but they were not at the address listed on the transfer papers.

It was in the dead of winter with ice on the ground. I finally located them in the median of Interstate 40 close to Sayre. Their vehicle had broken down and they had simply chose to stay there for a short time before moving into Sayre. I think they were waiting for someone in Arkansas to wire money.

I entered their travel trailer finding them without heat or water. The vehicle had been repaired, but they had not relocated, for some reason. I never understood why, but from what I observed that day, I didn't care. Their beautiful child was sitting on the floor crying; it didn't take long for me to understand why. The baby's clothing was frozen to the floor. I couldn't believe that her parents were just sitting there, covered up from head to toe while she was freezing to death.

I took the child and quickly wrapped her in my heavy coat. I told both of them if they said just one word, I would put them under the Beckham County Jail, not in it. Neither of them said a word. I also told them their transfer to the State of Oklahoma was denied because of their treatment of the child. I told them they had better be gone by the next day.

The child hung on to me when I gave her to child services. As I left, she started to cry again, as did I.

I never checked back with the court or DHS, but I'm sure the parents got the child back. They didn't deserve her.

I should have put this information under the heading "The Scum of the Earth."

PRESIDENT JIMMY CARTER

One of my more interesting activities while assigned to the Elk City area, was working a security detail with the Secret Service when President Jimmy Carter held a town hall meeting there in March, 1979. They had called me to request that I work with them because of my knowledge of the area and the people that could possibly be a security risk to the President. I considered it an honor to serve in a such a capacity.

Several other local law enforcement officers were invited to work security for the two days President Carter was in Elk City. We initially met for a security briefing where we were paired with Secret Service Agents or assigned a particular job to perform. Flyers were passed out including photographs and descriptions of those targeted as known trouble-makers for the President.

There was a long tractorcade made up of farmers unhappy with many things going on in the government. In fact, later in the year, there would be approximately 6000 farmers travel to Washington in a tractorcade in protest of American farm policy.

The protest at Elk City was peaceful as was the town hall meeting. Many questions that evening concerned farm products, while others had questions about inflation, energy prices, federal regulations, wage guidelines, abortion, military, the possibility of a draft, utilities and government aid.

The first night, we sat in a car all night in front of the location where the President stayed. It was relatively a quiet night until a farmer's tractor back-fired. We all scrambled thinking it was a gun shot. It was a huge relief to learn what caused the noise.

I was assigned to an Agent from Maryland who made sure I understood every detail of the security assignment. We also worked the town hall crowd; me, particularly, because I knew "the bad guys in town" they said.

I diligently weaved in and out of the crowd that night, looking for any possible threat to the President. A certain man caught my attention because he seemed to be doing the same thing, except, he didn't look like a local; I had also not seen him at the security briefing. He was wearing a long trench coat and an English driving hat. He was not wearing a pin on his jacket that we all wore to identify each other as law enforcement. The more I followed him, the more I thought I could detect a weapon under his coat. In fact, he could have been carrying anything under that coat.

I decided to contact the agent I had been assigned to and identified the man as a possible threat. Once we were in the holding room, which was set aside for interogation or investigation, other agents began to laugh. One said; "_____, you forgot to wear your pin today, didn't you?" He was an Agent with the Secret Service. I felt like an idiot until I was told "good job," by the agent I was with.

It was embarrassing beyond belief. I had worked for two days, then caught a Secret Service Agent. I didn't think it was so funny.

WHAT A PLACE TO HIDE

I have found people hiding in some strange places; the attic of a house, inside kitchen cabinets, in a roll of carpet, under a house, under a car, in the truck of car, in a tree (brilliant), in a farm pond (smart), closets, under a mattress (brilliant - think about the lump), and on top of a mountain. I'm sure there are others.

I had a Texas Parole Warrant for a women I had been supervising in Elk City. As we knew where she lived, an Elk City Detective and I had one of her friends (some friend) call her to make sure she was at home. When it was confirmed that she was, we drove to her house in less than one minute. We could not get her to come to the door, but used keys we had obtained from the owner to access the house. We began a search of the residence. We could also smell cigerette smoke, so we were certain the woman was in the residence. We searched everywhere; closets, attic, under beds, on top of this, under that; it simply didn't make sense. We even looked at the same places more than once. We were stumped.

As a last resort, I opened the dishwasher. There she was. She climbed out of the washer, put her arms around me and thanked me for saving her life. What a con. I handcuffed her, and of course, she began to cry.

The very serious aspect of this incident was, when she closed the dishwasher, the latch had secured the door. She would have died there, had I not found her. She had already pealed a section of the door gasket back in order to breath. However, she knew we were in the house searching for her and never made a sound. We found the dishwasher racks in tall weeds at the rear of the house, where she had thrown them.

She was very fortunate, but should be added to the "dumb crook files."

K-MART

K-Mart was one of the largest retailers in Elk City at he beginning of the oil boom. As a major employer in the area, benefits in sales and taxes were significant for the county.

Arden Dorney, a good friend of mine and a Detective for the Elk City Police Department, attempted to locate one of my probationers. I also searched for her because of an outstanding warrant. Neither of us were having any success in finding her, so we combined our resources.

She moved from residence to residence and rarely stayed in the same location more than one or two days, and also used another name. Within a few days, we learned that she had completed and filed an employment application at K-Mart, but under an assumed name. We decided to speed up the arrest process. We contacting K-Mart Management and made a rather unusual request. We asked for permission to present ourselves as K-Mart Management. When they agreed, we called the contact number she left and advised the contact person that her friend had been accepted for employment. We requested that she report for employment that particular morning.

Everything went according to plans until a black women who favored my client in her appearance, entered K-Mart. Officer Dorney made contact with her and advised of an outstanding warrant for her arrest. As she was not the person we were searching for, we received a rather interesting "cussing." We thought that was bad, until the right person came in; we then received a professional "cussing."

As I have always been taught, an arrest is an arrest, whether by deception or fraud, hook or crook. This would give the "blue light special" a completely new meaning.

EARLY ESCAPE

I believe I hold the supervision record for the shortest amount of time an inmate was on house arrest.

From time to time, out of necessity, the Oklahoma Department of Corrections establishes release programs to alleviate prison over-crowding. One of those programs was labeled "House Arrest." It was just another program to release inmates into the community earlier than normal, acting as a relief valve for the system. I always called the program "early escape," which the department did not appreciate.

House Arrest came with a set of rules which were very restrictive. Electronic monitoring was initially used as a method to monitor an inmate's activities and movements. Releases were restricted to the state, and normally, the county. The numerous rules and guidelines, were often more than the person could deal with, consequently, many were returned to confinement.

The longer house arrest was in effect, the more difficult it became to return them to confinement because of over-crowding. Unless they were a serious threat to the community or would simply not comply with rules, they remained in the community.

I was working out of Elk City at the time a young man from Hammon, Oklahoma was released on "House Arrest." I had supervised him previously and before he was sent to prison; I knew he had a severe alcohol abuse problem. His mother once advised me that he would take the fixtures out of her home, while she was gone, selling them in order to purchase alcohol.

The man stepped off a bus at the Elk City Police Department where my office was located, so drunk he could hardly walk. I immediately took him to the front and placed in a holding cell until I could return him to prison. I don't know how he managed to get alcohol on a bus, but he managed, somehow.

Where there is a will, there's a way.

A PAIR OF SLACKS

The Department of Corrections has experienced financial problems for as long as I can remember. Federal Court oversight, prison over-crowding, public opinion and state government's refusal to provide needed funding, were all legitimate reasons for correction's problems.

Probation and Parole has never escaped money problems when the rest of the department had difficulties. All correction's employees have experienced financial issues over the years, and all have faced times when they were required to take days off in lieu of wages.

I contacted one of my parolees in Hollis , finding another of my clients at the house. There was an outstanding warrant for the man, but he refused to submit to arrest and ran out the back door.

I was much younger in those days, and for a hundred yards, I could run with the best. One of my favorite comments to "runners" in those days, was, "If you run, you'll just go to jail tired." I pursued the man out the back door, temporarily losing him in some high weeds just outside. After walking around the area for a few minutes, I spotted him hiding behind a large tree, and the race was on again. He ran through an area of high weeds, across a creek and I lost him again. This time, I sat down behind some bushes and simply listened for the man to run again. I didn't wait long before he was on the move.

The young man was fairly fast. The only way I was able to get close to him, was when he fell as he crossed the creek. I was on top of the man trying to pull his arms up behind him, but I had mud on my hands from crossing the creek and could not hold him. He was up and gone again. He was faster than I was, and younger, but had apparently injured his ankle as he tried to jump across the creek. I caught up with him at a barbed-wire fence as he was trying to get on the other side. After a brief struggle, I was able to cuff him and we returned to my vehicle. I didn't mind the fact that my clothes were muddy, but the slacks I was wearing were torn from the knee to the waist band. They were ruined.

I submitted a claim to the Department of Corrections for the cost of replacing my clothing. They refused to reimburse me. After a few weeks, I re-submitted the claim, again requesting reimbursement for the pants. They again, refused.

At the end of the month, all officers submitted travel claims, or, at least those who sometimes drove their own vehicles. The cost of the slacks destroyed during my pursuit, was submitted again, but this time, in a different format. I told the finance officer; "There's a pair of slacks in there, somewhere, if you can find them." I did not enjoy that practice, but the department was obligated to reimburse me, and did.

THE PANTY THIEF

I supervised a variety of people during my career. Most were in what I would label as the "broad range" of normal, but there were many others who had almost unbelievable problems. I have supervised individuals who were pyromaniacs, others with different types of fetishes or an almost frightening list of phobias, burglars, forgers, murderers, child molesters, and a never-ending variety of other issues. One such client was a parolee from Texas, who had transferred his supervision to Oklahoma. He was a hard worker and caused few problems. The man also had a family.

In the Sayre area, for a period of several months, there had been someone breaking into residences taking only women's under garments - primarily, women's panties. Law enforcement had few leads to go on, no witnesses, no reliable evidence, and no suspects. It was beginning to create great fear for many in the county, especially women. Some were afraid to stay alone while others would not return home alone.

The State of Texas issued a Parole Revocation Warrant for my client due to a charge of Driving Under The Influence of Alcoholic Beverages. His original charge, for which he had gone to prison, also involved alcohol.

I arrested the man at his residence the day I received notification of the outstanding warrant. He presented no problems when arrested, although his wife, beat on the car windows all the way out of the driveway.

During booking at the county jail, the parolee was found to be wearing several pair of women's panties. Case solved, although I was somewhat surprised, as were others at the jail. I don't think I want to understand the man's reason for wearing women's under garments.

You never know about people.

PATTY LANIER

For many years, Probation and Parole Officers conducted background investigations on prospective employees. I recall the day I contacted Patty Lanier. She had completed college, worked for a short time at various jobs, then applied with Probation and Parole.

I had a somewhat different perspective when it came to women officers. I felt they had no business working in a male prison (I feel the same today) and had second thoughts of them working as a Probation and Parole Officer. I suppose my start with corrections in the prison system, the demand on officers to work closely with law enforcement and others reasons, made those impressions on me.

The address I went to was in Weatherford, Oklahoma. I Knocked on the front door and was greeted by a young girl; or so I thought. "Is your mother here?" I asked. Patty simply smiled and said, "No, I live here with my husband."

Ok, I know I had led a sheltered life, but this beautiful little girl, who appeared to be around 15 years of age, just couldn't be married, much less 21. But she was.

Patty's background was perfect, much to my disappointment, but all was not lost. I spent a great deal of time telling her how difficult the position was, the danger and physical demands. My pleas fell on very determined ears; she was in it for the "long-haul." Yes, I did my best to talk her out of going to work.

Patty, was soon accepted as a Probation and Parole Officer. She would go on to be one of the best officers I have ever worked with and, more importantly, a very close friend. She had an unusual affection for all animals, even skunks. It was impossible to stop and shoot a skunk when she was with me, but I would not stop to move a turtle out of the road.

In addition to an excellent officer and friend, she was always above reproach, always exhibiting a high degree of integrity. Those qualities are found in a small number of people in our society; her friendship is immeasurable.

RICHARD CARMICHAEL

Richard was one of the best men I have ever known. He left the Beckham County Sheriff's Department where he worked as Undersheriff, to work with Probation and Parole.

He was a giant of a man, in more ways than just his physical stature. He was compassionate, caring and a fine Christian man who loved his family. He and I became very close over the years. We were like brothers.

There was another side of Richard. I always thought God made him for law enforcement, especially investigative work. Nothing got by him; he just had a special gift of knowing people's hearts. His ability to understand a person's thoughts, plans and desires was simply uncanny. He was a special person because of his many unselfish actions, his love for God, his country, and family.

Before Richard was appointed to fill the District Supervisor's Position in District V, he and I worked together in Beckham County. It was an honor to work with him. I learned a great deal from him, the most important was to always treat people with respect, regardless of their actions.

Richard was forced into retirement after working a few years as District Supervisor. He did not fit the department's idea of a supervisor, plus, I always suspected, the director did not want an ex-law enforcement officer as a department head.

Richard was unyielding, but in a fair and impartial way. He was loyal to his people, was admired, loved and respected by them.

My friend died a few years ago, and is greatly missed, but I stay in touch with his two daughters as I promised him.

SCOTT BENTON AND CHRIS WATERS

There are a number of officers I had the privilege of working with over the years. Some more memorable than others, but most were good employees.

Scott and Chris were excellent Probation and Parole Officers to work with. They shared the office in Elk City, worked well with the police and sheriff's department and possessed a quality hard to find these days; integrity and pride in their work. Both were above reproach, honest, with strong principles and morals, without blemish. I would trust either of them with my life, and may have on occasion.

Although Scott tried his hand at law enforcement with the Custer County Sheriff's Department for a time, he returned to Probation and Parole. Still in District V, he is currently a Team Supervisor. Scott is a quality person and a good friend.

Chris was the Department's Parole Officer of the year during the time she worked in Oklahoma City. Her work was excellent.

I remember sitting on a stakeout for a few nights in Elk City, as I attempted to catch a parole violator who could run like a deer. She told me to come by and pick her up. When I picked her up, she had her tennis shoes on, ready to give chase. I never forgot that.

Like Patty, she was an animal lover, which is a good quality, but I recall an occasion when it got me in trouble. She saw two Cocker Spaniel puppies on the side of the road, and had to stop; someone had dumped the dogs. I held them while she called animal control in Elk City. By the time they arrived, I had fleas all over me.

My fears materialized one day when she announced, she had enough and was quitting to return to an old work position in Elk City. I was afraid she would "burn out" at some point, but the department lost a very quality officer when she left. She could never be replaced.

UNLICENSED SURGEON

Because the counties we worked shared common borders, Patty Lanier worked with me much of the time. She was a great help to me during the oil boom when I often had more than I could deal with. I also helped her when her workload was heavy.

Patty called one day asking that I come to Clinton and help her with a probationer. She said he was experiencing mental problems which prevented him from functioning as he should. She said there was something strange going on with him this particular day.

Patty was waiting near the probationer's mobile home when I arrived. She and I talked with the neighbors who were aware of problems the young man was experiencing. They advised that he had been up most of the night, practicing some type of martial arts. We could see he had broken several windows out of the mobile home. The neighbors knew of no weapons in his possession, however, said he could have knives or firearms and they would not be aware of the fact.

Patty and I decided to enter the trailer at the back door, which was unlocked. Upon entering, I could see that he was asleep on the couch in the living room. We quietly walked to that room, where I hoped to restrain the man before he was awake. As he began to stir, Patty was talking with him about the violations he had been committing. I was barely able to cuff the man, before he was fully awake.

Once the young man was in custody, there were several things in his residence that raised a red flag. There was a hand-drawn Physician's License/Diploma hanging on the wall, bearing his name. He had numerous surgical instruments scattered out over the living room, in addition to, dozens of medical books, journals and other medical publications. In one of the medical journals, there was a section marked and underlined dealing with appendectomies. When I frisked the young man for weapons, I found a diagram on his side (dotted lines) indicating he was preparing to remove his own appendix.

The probationer was taken to a mental health facility. Good grief, what was this man thinking?

STAKEOUTS

This was never my favorite thing to do, however, it was necessary from time to time. There are times more conducive to apprehending someone than other times. I have forfeited a few holidays to catch someone, knowing they would be with their family. I know, doesn't sound fair, does it; but there is nothing fair about this business.

Deputy Tim Scott and I were watching someone in northern Greer County, one afternoon, which I will not forget. We were taking turns watching the man through a pair of binoculars. If you have ever watched an object in this manner, then you know your vision presents a problem within a short time.

One of us, and I can't remember who, stepped off in a ditch trying to get a better view. We were both attacked by a swarm of Buffalo Gnats. If you are not familiar with these little devils, then you are fortunate. Buffalo Gnats, or black flies, are small humpbacked biting flies. They are extremely aggressive, even to the point of crawling into the nose, ears, eyes as they continue to bite. Humans are not exclusive contributors to these blood sucking flies, and there are over 100 species in North America. The extreme pain, itching and the local swellings, cause many problems for humans as well as domestic animals. Livestock and poultry are sometimes killed by large numbers of these pests. And, to make matters worse, their bites are magnified at certain times of the year. As luck would have it, the time of the year when the bites were much worse, probably started that day. As we tried to get back in our vehicle, our exposed skin took on the appearance of someone who had been shot with a shotgun.

The stakeout was over. It was time to get home and apply bleach to our wounds.

Chiggers, also known to many as harvest mites or red bugs, are extremely small and are not visible to the naked eye. If you have children who play outside during the summer months, then you are likely as familiar with chiggers as you are poison ivy or poison oak.

The chigger's bite is usually not felt. That is the reason you do not normally know of their presence until it is to late. Once the chigger learns that the first layer of your skin is a good place to feed, then you have a problem.

I was working with a Beckham County Deputy Sheriff in an attempt to catch an oil field thief. We were watching a location north of Elk City where someone had hidden several thousands of dollars in stolen oil field equipment in an abandoned storm shelter. We were actually waiting for the person or persons to return and retrieve the stolen property. We were hidden behind an old building on the farm site, watching the storm shelter where the stolen items had been stashed. We were standing (or sitting) in tall weeds behind this building. We, or course, didn't know we were being eaten alive, at least, not until we had returned home. Both of us began to itch and scratch uncontrollably before comparing notes. Soon after, we were both bathing in salt water, which is about the only reasonable method of dealing with chiggers.

No, we didn't catch the thief, only chiggers by the thousands all the way to the top of my head. Several hot, saltwater baths would do the trick.

So, be careful where you stand; stolen oil field equipment is not worth the pain.

COURT

If you think there are things in your life that are unpredictable, you should sit in district court for a few days. You will see things you never thought possible.

I think I have been in court in just about every county in Oklahoma, heard every stupid question asked by attorneys and could fill a book with the things I have seen or heard in courtrooms. I have fought with prisoners, chased escapees and helped officers pull a defendant off the presiding judge. I have escorted people to jail for contempt, at the request of the court, sat at the back of the courtroom with a carbine, at the judge's request, and gagged and "hog tied" a defendant who wouldn't shut his mouth. I have had some strange experiences in court.

I was on my way to a county in northern Oklahoma on a subpoena, to testify for the state and against a probationer. I was late, for some reason, and was speeding - I'm talking, speeding - in excess of 100 mph. As I topped a hill near Buffalo, I met an Oklahoma Highway Patrol Trooper. Knowing he would turn around on me, I pulled over at the bottom of the hill to wait. I could hear him coming and watched as he slid to a stop. I advised him of my reason for speeding and my need to get to court. When I told him who the defendant was, he said; "Hell, I arrested him. Let's go." I got my first escort to court, even faster than I had been driving.

This incident occurred in Beckham County District Court. I was on the stand, testifying for the state on a Motion to Revoke Suspended Sentence. The defense attorney was having a field-day as he cross examined me, with no objections from the Assistant District Attorney. When I glanced in his direction, I noticed that he had fallen asleep. I don't think the court thought it appropriate that I woke him by shouting out his name, but I needed some relief.

I was in court one morning in Greer County District Court waiting to testify in a criminal case. The young man in court was not a bad sort; he made poor decisions from time to time, but was not the type anyone would want in the prison system. His twin brother had posted his bond; I think it was on a forgery case.

Things were going well for the state and not so good for the defendant, when the young man decided he had enough and ran from the court room. Officer Tim Scott and I were right behind him, however, he appeared to have more incentive as he pulled away from us. Tim was shouting, "I'm going to kill you!". Each time he would shout, the defendant would start crying and running faster. If it had not been so serious, it would have been humorous.

We chased the man across the city square, west on Lincoln Street then south down an alley. Suddenly, a man passed both Tim and I, running the escapee down. When we got to them, it was the man's twin brother, the one who had posted his bond. He was now on top of his brother, hitting him in the face with everything he had.

As we pulled him off his brother, we could see the blood and tears on the young escapee's face.

A person can't run from problems, especially the ones inside a courtroom, and particularly when your twin brother has posted your bond and can outrun you.

In another case, one of my probationers was in court on a charge of murder when one of the witnesses leaving the witness stand spit in his face as she walked by. He went after her as a deputy and I tried to restrain him. We pulled him back turning over two courtroom benches in the process. I was on top of the defendant holding his arms across his chest. I will never forget his eyes, staring and blank with a slight quiver running through his entire body. I continued to ask him, "Are you alright?" His facial expression and vision were not normal for at least 30 seconds, when he finally said, "Yes". He had simply lost control.

As I looked around, the only people in the courtroom were Undersheriff Tim Scott who had restrained the witness who started the incident, the defendant, Deputy Sheriff Bill Buchanan, and me.

Emotions run high when life and death hang in the balance, especially in a homicide case.

BATS

When I had an office in Mangum, it was located on the second level of the Greer County Jail/Mangum Police Department Building. There were usually only a few inmates in the old jail, as most were held down stairs in the newer cells. The old building was constructed near the time of statehood, so you can only imagine its general condition.

I began to hear strange noises in the ceiling of my office, one day, and over the next few days, it grew worse. I attributed the disturbances to mice or rats, but after listening closely, I knew it had to be bats. They were beginning to get on my nerves. The bats were coming into the building through a crack located just over the east window in my office. Undersheriff Tim Scott and I watched them come and go in the late afternoon. We decided to rid the facility of the pesky devils.

On a slow day, we borrowed one of the city's bucket trucks with the bright idea of spraying "Pepper Spray" in the opening, thereby causing the bats to evacuate the premises. Sounded like a good plan. We didn't wish to harm the noisy little creatures; we were only interested in relocating them. It was a noble undertaking, but not without its flaws.

If you are not familiar with "Pepper Spray," you should be. The chemical is made from the fruit of plants in the Capsicum genus, including chilies (hot peppers). Also known as OC Spray, this non-lethal agent is carried by most police officers and is used to subdue combative individuals. Probation and Parole Officers also carry the agent in small, concealable canisters, used for the same purpose.

I remember when the spray first came out. I had an individual on parole who ran from the police, making it to his front yard. The police could not get him to submit to arrest, thereby offering a perfect opportunity to use this new chemical agent. Not knowing a great deal about it, they emptied two canisters on him before he finally simply fell over.

The next morning, I talked with him in jail. He looked like a boiled lobster. He said he would never resist arrest again, especially if officers were carrying pepper spray.

It can also be used on bears, dogs, for self-defense, crowd control and riot control. In rare cases, it can also be used to relocate bats (I just threw that in).

Having never experienced this chemical, you cannot comprehend the pain. As officers, we were required to "take a hit" in the face before being authorized to carry it. Instructors paired us up having the other officer try and take our weapon from us. I never gave up my weapon, but the officer I was paired with weighed about 300 pounds. He waved me around like I was a handkerchief. Blindness and the inability to get a breath of air sometimes causes the person to panic, but they are usually compliant. It simply hurts like hell; what other choice is there?

We raised the bucket to the window then emptied a canister of pepper spray into the opening. It was only a matter of seconds before the effects were noticed, however, not in the way we had anticipated. The bats came out alright, but they flew straight into the asphalt parking lot, somewhat reminiscent of Japanese kamikaze pilots. We were initially shocked at this method of "bat suicide" but realized we had actually murdered the little intruders. I suppose the spray disrupted their radar or ability to navigate.

We sealed the crack over the window promising never to use pepper spray on guests of the jail again, unless, of course, they were causing excessive noise.

RUN OUT OF TOWN

I have to admit, I occasionally violated department policy over the years. If policy conflicted with the communities well-being, I usually leaned toward the community.

A particular client, a transfer from Texas living in Sayre, was causing problems for people in the area. He scared the elderly as he would go to their homes begging for money or other things. He would not hold a job, would not accept assistance from the state and was what I would call "a nuisance." I attempted to work with him over a period of several weeks before taking another approach.

I received complaints from citizens, the sheriff's department and police department regarding this man's behavior. Although I had warned him numerous times, he continued to single out people who lived alone or individuals who were elderly, as he begged for money. Some of the people were so scared, they gave him money, or whatever he asked for.

I picked the man up one morning and drove him to the Texas/Oklahoma Stateline. I gave him some money, telling him never to come back to the state.

My new approach worked for Oklahoma, but he committed an armed robbery in the first town he came to in Texas. Of course, authorities there found my card in his pocket and called the Department of Corrections in Oklahoma. They advised my superiors that I had run the man out of the state; they also explained the incident in Texas.

I was contacted by our state office. I was asked about the circumstances of the "excommunication." I told them it was for the good of the community. Although they told me it was not a good idea, they understood. The man was born and raised in Texas.

I have done the same thing in Mangum, Elk City and Granite, but without consequences. When I began my employment with the department, my goal was always to protect the community. Although there are other considerations involved, that has always been my purpose in the work.

THE FARM WENT BROKE

The last few years I worked, there was an increasing trend that was very disturbing. Illegal drug manufacturing moved out of the big cities and into small communities and rural areas. During the increase in oil and gas exploration in Beckham County, authorities witnessed this phenomena as the number of drug manufacturing cases climbed. At the same time, the crime rate began to rise, as the two go together.

Methamphetamine, in particular, became the drug of choice. That dangerous compound is easy to transport, inexpensive to manufacture, and can be concealed easily. "Cookers" seemed to be plentiful in those days, as they also were leaving the urban areas for less populated locations.

Another illegal drug (marijuana) was also easily concealed, could be grown about anywhere, inexpensive and commonly used by many. I remember assisting the Beckham County Sheriff's Department, Elk City Police and The Drug Task Force with a raid in the south part of the county. Authorities had known about the operation for some time, but had only recently, obtained enough information for a search warrant.

There were about ten of us. The summer heat had risen to well over 100 degrees, with no wind. It was one of those "Western Oklahoma hot days." We surrounded the house, blocked any avenue of escape, then attempted to make contact with someone inside the house. We tried for about an hour to make contact, then began to make plans to enter the residence.

The vest I was wearing was heavy and hot. I finally removed it and laid it across a low limb on the tree I was standing behind. I thought it better to die of a gunshot wound than to overheat in the Oklahoma sun.

I will never forget entering the house. A coffee pot on the stove was still warm and numerous other items indicated someone had left in a hurry. There was a note on the table which read:

"The farm went broke, JD, get out of Dodge."

I felt like the sheriff in an old "B" Western, but, we had missed old "JD." We did, however, harvest his rather expansive marijuana crop. I have never seen marijuana that large, at least, not out in a field. Some of the larger stalks were so big, it took an axe to cut them. They were then placed on a flat-bed trailer, taken to a large pit and burned. And yes, we did stand upwind, most of the time.

JD would be caught, but not for more than a year.

PAINT SNIFFERS AND OTHER WILD ANIMALS

"Huffers," they are sometimes called - paint sniffers. These people are volatile and can be very dangerous to deal with. Whether it is paint thinner, gasoline, glue, or some other toxic compound, individuals who are involved in this type behavior are hooked and will "huff" about anything. There is a compound in spray paint (the propellant) that causes a person to become extremely violent and strong. Most retail stores selling paint, glue, or some other compound that can be used as an inhalant, keep them under lock and key. Many young people become involved in this extremely dangerous habit because the compounds are cheap and fairly easy to obtain.

Sniffing or "huffing" is an addictive habit that also causes great physical harm to the individual. The brain cells are destroyed very quickly with no chance of regeneration.

I have talked with people who sniffed substances for years, and, who are forever affected because of irreversible brain damage. The individuals can be identified easily by conversing with them. It takes a little longer for your questions or comments to register with them. It is like some of their circuits have been burned out, and that is precisely what has taken place.

I arrested one of my clients in Greer County on an outstanding warrant and took him to the county jail. He presented no problems when arrested, as he was compliant and cooperative. I could smell some type of fumes on the man, but he did not appear to be intoxicated.

Once I had him in the booking room at the jail, the Greer County Sheriff, Alfred Rogers, advised that his staff would book the prisoner. I left the building and drove to another location in Mangum, but the person I was trying to locate was not home. As I pulled back into the parking lot at the sheriff's office, I saw the man I had arrested, running out the front door with a police officer trying to hold him. The officer was trying to stop my client, but with little success. I left my vehicle blocking his path, as I attempted to talk to him. He began swinging wildly, trying to hit me in the face. He stood well over six-foot, much taller than me, but I was successful in dodging his blows. When I was satisfied he wasn't going to listen to me, I tried to subdue him. After he made a few swings and misses, I was able to get a solid wrist lock on him and take him to the pavement. Once he was restrained and back inside the jail, I learned that he had assaulted Sheriff Rogers and bruised one of his kidneys, which required hospitalization. I also tore some ligaments in my shoulder which would cause problems the rest of my life.

We never knew what set the young man off, causing him to assault someone, but I suspect it had something to do with paint sniffing.

MORE PAINT

I once had a client in Mangum who was what I would call a

"hardcore huffer." I could never get him away from that dangerous habit. He would sniff anything: gasoline, glue, paint thinner, but his favorite was gold spray paint. I couldn't count the times I have contacted him and found gold paint around his mouth or in his nostrils.

I was driving to work one morning and met him traveling in the opposite direction. But something was different this morning; he had a plastic bag pulled over his mouth and nose. I knew he was sniffing paint. I turned around on him but before I could stop him, he passed out in the middle of the highway.

Over the next several years, I lost contact with the man, but I would venture to say that, if still alive today, he is "huffing" something.

DON'T WRITE HOT CHECKS IN LEEDEY, OKLAHOMA

At that time, I was a field supervisor over the Woodward Office. I had spent most of the day there, but had stopped in Leedey for fuel, when I stumbled over one of Oklahoma City's wanted parolees.

I had stopped at a convenience store in Leedey and was in the process of refueling, when the store owner struck up a conversation with me. He had noticed the antennas on my vehicle, my badge and sidearm. After I explained who I worked for and what I did, he asked that I come into the store. Once inside, he presented me with several "hot" checks, written, he said, by an Oklahoma Parolee. He went on to say that the man and his family had left town several weeks ago.

I took one of the checks, ran the man through NCIC, made a few inquiries in the area and learned where the family had previously lived. The family had children who had been in the Leedey School System prior to their disappearance. I contacted school officials thinking there might have been a request for school records. I was correct. Only a few days before, a small school in south Texas had requested the children's school records.

I contacted the sheriff's department in the county in Texas and advised them of the outstanding warrant. I suggested that Texas officials follow the children home as they left school.

I left Leedey, but before I was out of the county, I was contacted by Texas officers; they had arrested the parolee after following the children home.

I contacted Probation and Parole in Oklahoma City to let them know of their parolee's apprehension. I couldn't believe it when they asked if I would go to Texas and return the individual to Oklahoma. I thought that took a lot of nerve, especially after I tracked the man down for them.

I actually told them where they could go and it wasn't Texas, although, I suspect, it is also warm there.

Sometimes things work out, sometimes they don't.

COCKLEBURS

I made several arrests during the oil boom in Elk City. Most were uneventful, but sometimes, there was a foot pursuit or wrestling match. This would be one of those days.

I was driving through the Elk City Park one day when I noticed one of my parolees as passenger in a vehicle. I stopped the young man and advised both to get out of the vehicle. They both complied with my instructions, but the parolee advised he knew he was in trouble. He was correct. There was a department of corrections parole revocation warrant outstanding for his arrest. He had disappeared from Elk City several months before without contacting me for permission. He had not reported in over a year. I advised the parolee that he was under arrest and requested that he turn around and put his hands behind him. He refused to comply, and suddenly ran.

The young man, who was driving the car, presented an immediate problem. I had to advise him of possible charges against him if he chose to pick his friend up.

By the time I had explained the situation to the driver; my parolee was out of sight. I contacted the Elk City Police requesting assistance. It was less than a minute before an officer showed up and we began to drive through the area searching for the escapee. I had watched him run across old Highway 66 south of the City Park, but had no idea where he had gone.

We drove around for a few minutes before I spotted the man as he ran between two houses, however, I lost him again. Another few minutes went by then, I spotted him again. This time, he was hiding under a bridge that crossed a dry wash. The Elk City Officer and I drove off into the wash on each side of the bridge. As the parolee ran toward me, I leveled my weapon at him over the top of the car and ordered him to get on the ground. He turned and ran in the opposite direction, back under the bridge, then out the other side. The Elk City officer shouted; "I'm going to shoot you!" That made an impression on the man because he dove into a patch of brown, ripe cockleburs. That was not a smart move. He was wearing only a pair of cut-off jeans, no shirt or shoes.

I was on top of him within seconds and as he was still screaming. As I jerked his left arm behind him, he shouted; "You broke my arm again!" Having never broken the man's arm before, I didn't understand what he was saying.

When I had him restrained, I helped him to his feet. He was covered with brown cockleburs from his head to his ankles. I removed as many as possible. By the time I got him to the Beckham County Jail in Sayre, he was miserable, still complaining about the cockleburs and the fact that I had broken his arm. I told him he shouldn't have run.

I was later told that his arm was broken; in the same place it had been broken previously. I know some of the cockleburs are still with him today, but, in my opinion, he was lucky he wasn't shot. I simply had difficulty feeling sorry for him.

MENTALLY DISTURBED

I accompanied Greer County Deputy Sheriff Frank (Bo) Smith to a disturbance call in south Mangum. The call that came into police dispatcher, Mike Rogers, involved a man and woman breaking windows out of houses. The caller also said the man had run them out of their home.

Frank and I arrived at the location and found the man standing just off the road. An elderly couple standing outside their house pointed to the man as the one who ran them out of their house. He had also broken windows out of the house, they said, for no reason.

I should point out that Frank is a black man and was one of the best law enforcement officers I have ever worked with. As we approached the man, he said; " I wonder how many "black bucks" it would take to put me in jail?"

He got his answer very quickly as Frank and I grabbed him, cuffed him and stuffed him in the back seat of our vehicle. When he began to complain about the tightness of the restraints, he was easily ignored.

Mangum police officers had arrived and were trying to get the woman (reported in the call to police) out of a house across the street. As Frank and I looked on, the woman came running from the house screaming as loud as possible, laid her baby on the ground and attacked 3 police officers. They were going around and around with her as she started kicking them like a wild animal. I saw her kick the chief of police in the groin and another officer in the stomach.

I was running across the street shouting at them to get the woman on the ground. I'm not sure if it had anything to do with Murphy's Law, but I ran through a huge mud puddle as I crossed the street, filling both shoes with water and mud. As I was approaching what appeared to be a 3-ring circus, the woman had her back to me. I took her to the ground, mud and all. I pushed her face into the ground until she stopped screaming. She was screaming again before we got them to jail. She was making sounds similar to a wild animal.

We would later learn that the man and woman we arrested were brother and sister. They were just out walking when they decided to break windows out of houses, for no reason. They were not on drugs, not intoxicated, just insane. Both, obviously, had mental problems and were treated accordingly.

Another pair of slacks ruined. Where do these people come from and why do we need them?

IT'S NOT YOUR HOUSE

I never quite understood this incident. Why would anyone do something like this?

A Beckham County Deputy was sent on a call to the west area of Sayre, and with no backup, I went along with him. The call indicated a man walked into a house, ran the owner and his wife out, then lay on the couch.

When we arrived, the elderly couple were standing outside with bewildered expressions. They told us the young man walked into their house, unannounced, without knocking and ordered them out. They didn't observe a weapon.

We entered the house and found a man lying on the couch. He appeared to be a transient, wearing military type clothing, was unshaved and dirty. He appeared to be asleep.

We tried to wake the intruder, finally sitting him up. As he began to come around, he leaned forward and I pulled 10-inch knife from the small of his back. At about the same time, he reached for the knife - where it had been. After the deputy saw the knife I was holding and watched as the man tried to grab it, he hit the transient so hard, it knocked him unconscious. In fact, we had to carry him to the deputy's cruiser.

Keep your doors locked.

A COLD WINTER

My Mother always taught me "cleanliness is next to Godliness." I have tried to live by her words of wisdom regardless of the type work I performed. I was also fortunate to have married a woman who believed in the philosophy, carrying on where my Mother left off.

As a parole officer, many homes I visited were filthy, for lack of a better term.

In the late 1970's, I accepted a transfer from the state of Kansas. The man was an oil field worker, drawn to the area because of employment. He was living alone in an abandoned farm house near Sweetwater. The way he was living was appalling.

On my first visit to his house, the weather had turned cold. There was a strong, northerly wind that seemed to blow through the old structure with ease. There was, obviously, no insulation in the old farm house. When I entered the residence, the strong smell of smoke was the first thing I encountered. The second was the tree limbs and metal, 55 gallon barrel in the living room. He was in the process of cutting some tree limbs into small lengths which would fit into the barrel, which was his stove. There were dried tree limbs scattered throughout the room making it difficult to walk without tripping or falling. The man was dirty; his clothes were filthy. The whole scene was something less than desirable.

I was aware of the man's prior record, then, the .22 caliber rifle sitting in the corner caught my eye. As a parolee and a felon, he was in violation of his release rules by having the weapon. As I advised him of the violation, he admitted that he was aware of the infraction, but the weapon was only used for varmints around his place. He further stated that his father had given him the weapon. I advised him to have his father remove the weapon from the residence. I checked the rifle, found it loaded and gave him until my next visit to get rid of the gun.

My next visit was about the same as the first, except the smoke in the house was so thick, I had him step outside. I removed the rifle from the residence and placed it in the truck of my vehicle. I advised him that I would be filing a violation report to the state of Kansas because of his possession of a weapon. He said he didn't give a damn what I did. Great attitude.

By the next morning, the man was gone and the Sweetwater Grocery Store had been burglarized during the night. Apparently, he needed food for the road.

Kansas authorities were notified and the case was closed.

This was not an uncommon occurrence. Many men came to the oil fields, thinking it would be easy money, then became disillusioned when they found the work hard and dangerous. Opening and closing cases was an every day practice, however, not many of the men took half a grocery store with them as they left town.

"HOW IN THE HELL DID YOU FIND ME?"

I believe all officers have a few cases that make them want to pull their hair out. I have had many, over the years, but this would be my most challenging.

The man lived in Carter, Oklahoma, at the time, and was a constant thorn in my side. He usually stole from the community, but wouldn't pass up a chance to use illegal drugs.

With several thefts in the community where he lived, I began to look at this individual closely. By the time I began to put a few leads together, he had disappeared.

I had a cousin (Sidney Vanzandt) who advised the man I was searching for had stolen a checkbook out of his vehicle. The account was a money market account out of Boston, Massachusetts, providing me with further leads. I began tracking my parolee by the forged checks as they began to show up.

Eugene Hopper was working for the Beckham County Sheriff's Department as the Undersheriff and canine officer. He had retired from the Oklahoma Highway Patrol after 15 years.

Eugene and I were both trying to locate my parolee; I had a warrant for his arrest on a parole violation and Eugene wanted him on a county warrant. We had discussed the case several times, but neither of us had time to actively look for him.

One weekend, we decided to try and locate him. Eugene borrowed his grandmother's old car (it had a burned valve), we put on our jeans and ball caps and took off. The first lead we had came from the Norman, Oklahoma area, however, we learned that he had moved on. We continued traveling east, following up on leads, and by following the checks he was writing.

I think it was midnight, when we arrived in McAlester where we contacted law enforcement with the sheriff's department. I remember Eugene and I sitting in their office providing them with names of individuals who could possibly be hiding our fugitive.

143

Each time we mentioned someone, one of the deputies would respond by saying, " I'm not going out there, those people will kill you." After a few of those comments, we left.

After a few hours, we developed more information on the individual which led us into Coal County.   There, we were fortunate to find two young and eager deputies who assured us they would go anywhere we needed them. That was a bright spot in our day, especially in eastern Oklahoma at 2:00 in the morning.

Our latest information took us to a home-site on top of a pine covered hill - I think the people there refer to them as mountains - which required that we walk approximately a quarter-mile. Luckily there was a bright moon that helped us a great deal, although it was still difficult to navigate through the brush and tree stumps. We tried not to use our flashlights.

The old house and out-buildings reminded me of something out of the movie, "DELIVERANCE,"   minus the actors, of course. The light breeze made a humming sound as it drifted through the tall pine trees covering the top of the mountain. Sounds from the crickets, frogs and other night creatures made a person feel closer to nature, and more importantly, to God. It was a very peaceful time, but there were things to do.

The old gentleman we got out of bed was pleasant enough, at such an hour, but was somewhat shocked to see us on his property. We presented him with a photograph of the individual we were searching for, which he quickly identified as the person cutting wood for him. He pointed at a small travel trailer parked in some trees about a hundred yards from his house, as he said, "He's staying out there, good worker."

 Eugene and I walked to the small camper and walked through the unlocked door.   Our fugitive was sprawled out on a couch sound asleep.   Eugene kicked the side of the couch as he announced, " Hey, get up, we've got a long way to go." I have never seen a look on anyone's face to equal our wood cutter. His mouth fell open slightly as he looked up at us and said, "How in the hell did you find me?" We just rolled him over and cuffed him.

Once outside, I located the man's vehicle and started a quick search. I found 20 to 25 stolen credit cards in the glove compartment, most of which had been taken from the Elk City area. I also found the check book stolen from Sidney Vanzandt with numerous practice signatures in the back. There were other items in the vehicle which appeared to have been stolen.

I think it was well up into the morning when we returned to Sayre with our prisoner. Later, our fugitive was charged with several felonies, after former conviction of a felony, and his parole status was revoked. He received a substantial sentence.

I recall being at the Oklahoma State Penitentiary for a parole revocation hearing a few years later and ran into my former parolee. I think he must have been assigned as a maintenance worker in the administrative building. When we met, he said, "Paul, you don't really like me much, do you?" My reply was, "I sure wouldn't want you dating one of my daughters."

GIRL SCOUT MURDERS

One of Oklahoma's worse homicides occurred June 13, 1977, at a girl scout camp near Locust Grove, Oklahoma. Three young girls, ages eight, nine and ten, were found murdered just outside the camp in a field, after being dragged from their tent. This horrific and savage taking of three young lives would spark one the largest man-hunts in the history of Oklahoma.

Almost immediately, the search for the killer focused on Gene Leroy Hart, a former high school football star from the area. Hart, a full blood Cherokee Indian, was sentenced in 1966 for kidnapping two women outside a Tulsa nightclub, raping them and leaving them tied up in the woods to die. They were able to free themselves and report the crime, as well as the suspects tag number.

Hart was released on parole in 1969, burglarized several homes and returned to prison. He was transferred to Pryor, Oklahoma in 1973 as a result of a post-conviction relief hearing, when he escaped from custody. He was captured and escaped again, but this time, he was not caught.

Hart showed up in Locust Grove, was seen by many people, but because of his Indian heritage and family and friends there, he was able to avoid capture. Following the murders of the three girl scouts, he became the suspect, triggering an intense man-hunt.

A cave was located in the area, with photographs found by investigators. Those photos were placed on National Television in hopes that someone would recognize them. My wife and I identified the pictures as being residents of Greer County in Southwest Oklahoma and notified the OSBI. They requested that I wait for two agents in Mangum.

It was pouring rain that night and I remember laying down in one of the cities jail cells to get some sleep. Once the two agents arrived, which was very early the next morning, I took them to the homes of those people identified in the photos. The pictures were of local women, taken at a wedding reception. It was quickly determined that the photographs were developed at the Oklahoma State Reformatory by Gene Leroy Hart, when he was imprisoned there. The records officer, often took photos for weddings and other formal gatherings, brought the film back to the reformatory and had Hart develop them in the prison dark room. Hart had, obviously, made himself extra photos of these women.

The search for Hart continued with more than half the state's OSBI Agents assigned to the highly publicized case. There was an enormous amount of evidence against Hart, but it would be some time before he was captured because family and friends were willing to hide him.

When Hart was located and arrested, he was tried for the murders of the three young scouts. Picking a jury in the Cookson Hills area would prove to be very difficult as Hart had become somewhat of a folk hero. There was also the fact that he was a full blood Cherokee Indian with family and friends in the county.

He was found not guilty of the murders, however was returned to prison to serve the remainder of his original sentence. He would die of a heart attack while in prison; at least that was the official cause.

Our criminal justice system has its flaws, but is still the best in the world. When we, as citizens, see injustice in our courts, we often forget how truly effective the process really is. It may not punish all those brought before it, but, there remains a higher power to consider. We will all stand before God some day to answer for each thing we have done in this life, whether good or bad. I would hate to be in Hart's shoes on that day.

Black Sunday

"Dirty 30s"

The Mauldins
Tuff, Ruff, Mrs. Mauldin, Taught, Raught

John H. "Shorty" Johnson
My Grandfather

Roscoe, Paul
First Irrigation Well
1958

Paul, David, Roscoe

Paul and his Pig

Linda and Paul's Wedding
1962

Shannon and Linda
On the farm

Calvin Vanzandt

Paul and Linda

Roscoe and Ernest

Richard Carmichael
And Family

Shawn Laughlin and Tim Scott
Disposing or Imbibing ?

Peggy and George Roach
Caprock Canyon
Texas

Linda and Paul Morris
Caprock Canyon
Texas

Nathan and Connor Wood

Joan Morris
My Mother

District V Enid
"Early Years"

My Girls
Sharra, Shannon, Linda

Shannon, Chris, Nathan, Connor Wood
And Friends

Chris, Shannon, Wood

Elk City Range
Chris Frech, Terry Jantz, Patty Lanier, Ed Wrather, Jerry Graybill

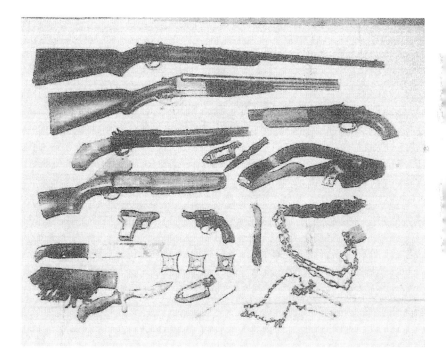

Oil Boom

Sharra and Paul
College
Graduation

First Car
1954 Chevrolet

Paul and Linda
2006 Cruise

Patty and Bob Lanier
And daughters

July 4th
Sharra, Shannon, Paul

President Carter
Elk City

Paul and Linda
Retirement
2000

ALBERT "CREEL" GASTON, WOODWARD COUNTY SHERIFF

You have probably heard the old saying, "in the wrong place at the wrong time." I am living proof of that statement.

In addition to my own caseload, I was a field supervisor in 1982, supervising two officers in the Woodward County Office. I was in the process of auditing case files in the Woodward Office when we were advised the County Sheriff, Creel Gaston, had been shot while conducting an investigation. We joined the search for the two men responsible.

According to reports, Sheriff Gaston was investigating the theft of gasoline when he spotted a vehicle matching the description of the individuals involved. As the sheriff approached the vehicle, he was shot once in the chest with a .38 caliber pistol. The bullet penetrated a lung, lodging next to his spine, paralyzing him from the waist down.

The weather in Southwest Oklahoma has always been very unpredictable, but this particular day in January, was a day I will never forget. The wind was blowing at gale force, it was snowing off and on, and it was bitterly cold. I learned the hard way to always carry appropriate clothing when in the field, and my old down-filled coat felt like a million dollars.

We began searching barns and abandoned home-sites in the general area of Woodward. It was a major relief to search a building and get out of the harsh weather.

Officer Lee Crowe and I were together as the search began. Crowe had worked only a short time with us, however, he was a 20 year veteran police officer having recently retired from the State of South Carolina. I could tell he knew the business well as we began to stop individuals on the roads and streets, question them and conduct a cursory search of their vehicles. He would, however, be terminated from his position after only a short time with the department, due to numerous violations of department policies.

David Behrens was apprehended, following the shooting and was later convicted. He received a 144 year prison term.

Sheriff Gaston recovered from his wound enough to complete the last two years of his term in office, but, from a wheelchair. He would suffer long term complications from the shooting and died in 1986 from pneumonia. He was 70 years old.

Gaston was a good officer and a fine individual. He literally gave his life for his community, as many have done over the years.

It was a tough day for all of us, but especially, for the Gaston family.

RICHARD NORMAN ROJEM

Richard Norman Rojem was born December 19, 1957. He was convicted in Macomb County Michigan in 1979 for the crimes of Criminal Sexual Conduct 1st Degree, 3 counts, and Criminal Sexual Conduct 2nd Degree, Count 4, receiving a sentence of 6 to 15 years with the Michigan Department of Corrections. Once released on parole, he successfully transferred his supervision to the State of Oklahoma in July, 1982.

Rojem was living with his wife, Mindy Lynn Rojem and her two children in Sayre, Oklahoma where he was employed as an oil field worker.

There were indications of on-going problems between Rojem and his wife almost immediately. They had physical altercations, but never serious enough to constitute an arrest. He once asked that I send him back to prison because he had assaulted Mindy, but she admitted striking him first.

After a few months of supervision, I received what I felt to be reliable information that Rojem was carrying a pistol. On January 22, 1983, I interviewed a young woman who was employed at C & G Quick Trip Convenience in Sayre. She reported Rojem was in the store that date and announced: "This is a stick up" and produced a handgun, pointing it at her. She said she personally knew him and told him her boss was in the back and he had better put the gun up, which he did.

Kermit Carter, co-owner of C & G Quick Trip advised he observed Rojem through a one-way mirror, putting a blue-steel handgun back into his waistband. Joe Bob Grisham said he also saw Rojem with a handgun pointing it at the clerk. Before he and his partner could do anything, Rojem had put the gun up and left the store.

Rojem claimed that a friend he was with actually had the gun when they entered the store and intended to rob it. He further claimed to have no knowledge of his friend having a firearm, but I learned that Rojem had recently purchased a shoulder holster for his friend. Rojem also said that he and his friend had been drinking that day and had gone into the convenience store in order to purchase additional beer.

On February 3, 1983, suspecting sexual conduct between Rojem and his seven year old step-daughter, Layla Cummings, I requested that Mindy bring both her children to the Beckham County Sheriff's Department. She complied with my request bringing both her children; Layla Cummings and her brother Jason. It was a difficult interview, because of the nature of the subject and the ages of the two children, but with the help of Beckham County Deputy Sheriff Florence Denton, Layla admitted that Richard Rojem had made her get into bed with him while he was naked. He would rub against her and make her perform oral sex on him.

I immediately contacted the Assistant District Attorney in Beckham County requesting charges be filed against Rojem. He felt that the young girl could not testify in court and refused to file charges. My only avenue was to request a warrant on his parole status and conduct a probable cause hearing, which I did. Because of the numerous violations against him, he was ordered returned to the State of Michigan where he would be incarcerated on his original charge.

I took Rojem from the Beckham County Jail and met a private transport plane at the Elk City Airport for his return to Michigan. As I was exchanging restraints with security personnel at the airport, Rojem advised that an individual in the Beckham County Jail had put out a "death contract" on my life in the amount of

$100,000.00. I never understood why he volunteered that information, but I was grateful. I would later pull two of my probationers out of jail and interview them regarding Rojem's claim. They both verified his statement.

The State of Michigan held Rojem for approximately six months before releasing him again. He did not request to come back to the area I supervised, but to Washita County, supervised by Harlan Ross. Harlan and I made every effort to deny his return to Oklahoma, but because he had work and was not living with his wife and her children, the Department of Corrections allowed him to return. This was done over the objections of both Harlan and I.

On July 7, 1984, Harlan and I were notified that Layla Cummings had been kidnapped from her mother's home in Elk City. We both knew immediately who had taken her and we raced toward Elk City. Before I could get there, I received directions to a wheat field near Burns Flat, Oklahoma. I knew what that meant.

When I arrived, there were several officers at the location. Harlan was already at the scene. Seven (7) year old Layla Dawn Cummings lay face down in the wheat field in her mother's nightgown. She had been abducted from her home in Elk City, taken to this deserted location, raped then stabbed in the neck and vaginal area. Her buttocks skin was torn, probably by fingernail scratches. There was also blunt force trauma to her hymen, but no sperm were found in her body. Her panties had been removed and stuffed in her mouth. A farmer had found the body that morning and notified authorities.

This was probably the worse day of my life. A beautiful little girl tortured beyond imagination then brutally murdered. It was an overwhelming situation. Harlan had almost lost control. He had worked diligently trying to keep Rojem out of Oklahoma. He had written letters to legislators and contacted several people, but no one had offered assistance. I feared he would hit the Assistant District Attorney that morning before I could get him to one side.

We told other officers at the scene that we were going after Rojem, but the OSBI asked that they be allowed to pick him up. I think they were afraid Harlan might lose control during the arrest.

Once Rojem was picked up, I talked with him at the Burns Flat Police Department. He had an attorney present and had been advised of his rights. I asked for permission to search his apartment, although I had the authority to search without his permission. He refused saying "you might find a little marijuana and revoke my parole." I quickly wrote out a statement and signed it indicating a small amount of marijuana found in his apartment would not constitute a parole revocation. He was so vain, he would not back up and agreed to the search.

Several incriminating items were located during the search of Mindy Rojem's property, the wheat field and Richard Rojem's apartment. It was also determined at a later date, that he had made attempts to manipulate possible evidence in the case.

Richard Norman Rojem was subsequently convicted by a jury in Washita County of first degree rape, kidnapping and murder of seven year old Layla Dawn Cummings. He received the death penalty for the murder and 1000 years imprisonment for both the kidnapping and rape. He has been on death row at the Oklahoma State Penitentiary since that time. He has only recently been re-sentenced to death for the 3rd time since his confinement, due to numerous filings with higher courts.

I have watched this case closely for several years. I think the system failed in this case from beginning to the present time. I also believe our criminal justice system's flaws cost a young girl her life, and the life of her father who later committed suicide. This case will haunt me for the remainder of my life. It will also affect Harlan Ross, who had a daughter about the same age as Layla.

Rojem continues to be held on death row while filing one appeal after another. The faceless little girl lying in the wheat field doesn't seem to be a factor any longer, as the system focuses on the rights of a man who would kill again if released.

I worked as an officer and supervisor for more that 30 years and have seen all types of offenders, but this man is, by far, the most dangerous individual I have ever supervised. He is as pure a sociopath, with no redeeming qualities, as I have witnessed in all my years as an officer. As far as I am concerned, he has forfeited his rights and should have been executed years ago.

THE MISSING BODY

Granite, Oklahoma is sheltered on the north by the last, westerly formations of the Wichita Mountain Range. It is a sleepy little farming community of approximately 1500 people, little crime and still, many unlocked doors. Although, not as safe as 20 years ago, it is still a good place to live and raise a family. If you need a vehicle, the keys are probably in the ignition, although I'm not advocating vehicle theft.

The mountains, to me, have always been a place of solitude. I have experienced a feeling of being nearer to God when on Mt. Walsh or one of the smaller mountains. My family and I have spent many hours in the mountains, searching for wild flowers, crawfish (during the rainy seasons), picnicking, and simply enjoying the scenery. We have assigned names to many formations in the mountains, feeling a personal connection to many locations. But that all changed one summer.

Tim Scott, Greer County Undersheriff, and I, began getting reports that a man had been murdered and his body hidden in the mountains. Normally, this would have simply been dismissed, however, I had received the same report from 3 sources and Tim had also received the same information from different individuals. There was simply too much information to dismiss.

We began to search the mountains, caves, water holes, under brush piles, old quarry pits and abandoned wells. We put divers in a large quarry excavation that had held water for many years. I recall Richard Williams and Jerry Nelson going into the ice-cold water at the abandoned quarry. Richard dove to the bottom and came up with a white catfish; it had never seen light. Nothing else was found.

We even drained a hand-dug well on the west side of the mountains as we searched for the body. I think we climbed around in the Wichitas for about a week before we had to get back to our regular work.

In a few weeks, after we had given up on the search, I located the man that was reported murdered. He was in a northern state and I talked with him by telephone. Because he could answer questions that only he would have known, we called off the search.

It was very strange and highly unusual to receive the same report from so many different people, then determine it was not true. At least, Tim and I built up our leg muscles and got some fresh air.

TWICE - CENTER MASS

I had been ordered to conduct a Pre-sentence Investigation on an individual in Beckham County who had plead guilty to robbing a local jewelry store. During my initial interview with the young man, he began to cry. I asked why he was crying and he responded, "Mr. Morris, I didn't rob that jewelry store." When I asked about his reason for pleading as he did, he said he didn't know why he did it. He said, "My cousin, who's retarded, is the one who did it."

Needless to say, I was somewhat shocked at this revelation. Usually, at this point in a case, the defendant has either plead guilty or has been determined guilty by the court. I got the man's name, terminated my interview and drove to his residence. The young man was living with his parents, more than likely, because of his mental state.

I asked to speak to the man, and he walked outside and approached me. This will be as close to our conversation as I can recall:

"My name is Paul Morris. I'm a Probation and Parole Officer with the State of Oklahoma. I've been visiting with your cousin about the jewelry store robbery. He said you robbed it. Is that true?"

"Yea, I robbed it."

"Were you going to let your cousin take the rap for you?"

"I don't know."

"What do you think should to done?"

"I don't know."

I could see no reason to continue my interview. I drove to the Beckham County Courthouse, talked with the District Judge, the Assistant District Attorney and got the charges dropped on the defendant. With the information I had, the District Attorney's Office was in the process of filing charges on the guilty man.

A few months following this incident, the young man I literally saved from going to prison, was in a standoff with police because of some type of domestic disturbance. He had a knife in each hand, refusing to comply with police instructions, but was trying to get them to find me. I was not available and after a few minutes, the man grew even more agitated and confused . At that point, he chose to commit "police suicide" by rushed the police officers. Both officers shot the man twice, I was told.

I had helped train both officers on the firing range. I know they had no choice in what they had to do, but one of them later said to me, "I shot him twice, center mass, just like you taught us."

I didn't even know how to respond; talk about mixed emotions....I still have them.

SEXUAL MOLESTATION OF A CHILD

I have always had difficulties working with individuals who had molested children. In my opinion, sexual molestation of a child should carry the same punishment as murder, regardless of the age of the offender. In the time I have worked as a field officer, I have seen many offenders in this category who usually re-offended. The numerous sex offender programs offering very high statistics on individuals who complete their programs and never re-offend, are manipulating figures. Most sex offenders can never break the mold, continuing to pose a threat to the public. That is the reason for sex offender registration. Do you know of another crime that requires such close scrutiny?

Although several sex offender cases come to mind, I remember the Interstate Transfer in Elk City during the oil boom. He had difficulty locating and maintaining employment because of his crime of Child Molestation. He was constantly on the move up and down the streets during the day as well as the nights.

I must admit, I did not supervise him as closely as I should have, but with the number of other cases I had, it was impossible. I simply did not have the time.

I was working in Elk City in the afternoon, when I was notified of the molestation of two small children who lived in the same general area of this offender. When I arrived at his residence, I was quickly advised by his neighbor, that he was the person who was babysitting the children that morning. I almost lost it. How could anyone in their right mind leave their two small children with a child molester? Are people crazy? I told the children's mother she should also be charged. She knew of the offender's background.

I went directly to the man's apartment, which was in the same building. I don't think I have been that angry, at least not since I began working with the Department of Corrections. I didn't bother knocking on his door, instead, I kicked the door as hard as I could and watched as it crashed back against the wall. I didn't hear the glass break, but I learned later that the door knob on the inside had come off the spindle, flying through the window and falling on the sidewalk in the front yard. All I wanted, at that time, was to get my hands on the man who had molested the two children. It was fortunate, for both of us, that he was on the run.

I checked with several sources and learned that he had left Elk City, because of what he had done. I placed the individual on NCIC as a wanted person and waited. I had no idea where he was or where he was going.

Within a few days, I received at "hit" on my probationer from the state of Florida. According to police, he was walking down the street in a small town in Florida when an individual drove his vehicle fairly close to him and he yelled out some obscenity. The man in the vehicle heard the comment and turned around. This time, he drove very close to the man, and, the probationer pulled a large knife and slashed out toward the vehicle taking a long strip of paint from the driver's side.

It was simply not his day; the entire incident occurred in front of the local police department, with several officer as witnesses. He was immediately arrested and found to be wanted in the state of Oklahoma.

Upon my client's return to Oklahoma, he plead guilty to the offense of Child Molestation, two counts and was sentenced to a lengthy prison term with a Hold placed on him from the sending state.

For several months, following this incident, I assumed some of the blame for the crimes against the children. Even though the parents of the children were aware of the previous charges against my client, I felt I was, in someway, partly responsible. I had no reason for my feelings and after a few months, was able to put it out of my mind. I think I was simply so angry, I blamed everyone, even myself.

"I'M CRAZY"

An enigma; that is my best effort at describing exhibitionism. Flashing, Lady Godiva Syndrome, apodysophilia are just a few of the terms identifying this strange compulsion. Not normally to be confused with indecent exposure, it is a psychological need to expose one's private parts to someone who is really not the least bit interested. I simply cannot understand this crime.

I supervised an exhibitionist in a small town in one of my counties. In a one-man office, there is no picking or choosing when it comes to certain crimes; I did it all.

I received a call from the Sheriff's Department in Sayre early one morning. I was advised that after receiving several calls from the public reporting a naked man standing on Interstate 40, they sent a deputy to the location. The deputy spotted my exhibitionist standing on the shoulder of the east-bound lane of Interstate 40, a few miles east of Sayre, Oklahoma. When the deputy stopped and approached the man, he asked, "What in the hell do you think you're doing out here without any clothes?" My client answered, "Well, I'm crazy."

The man was standing there without anything covering any part of his body. As my Mother used to say, "Naked as a Jaybird". He was watching the traffic go by, obviously enjoying the occasional honk, whistle or wave. He was in his element. The deputy arrested the man and took him to jail.

Although there are programs available for this type offense, intensive, long term treatment is the only alternative and few individuals are willing to invest that much time. Therefore, it will continue to be a problem.

WE ARE WHAT WE EAT?

We have all heard this statement, usually from health professionals or our Mothers, who inform us of a better and healthier way to eat. I'm sure you have all been exposed to horror stories of food eaten by different cultures. I can attest to one such horror story.

Estimated at eight-percent, Oklahoma has the largest population of Native American Indians of any other state. Before whites moved to settle the area, it was home to several Native American Indian Tribes.

Hammon, Oklahoma is located in Roger Mills County, a few miles north of Elk City. The American Indian population in that small town of approximately 500, is higher than in most communities in the state - about 37%.

During the oil boom in the 1970s and 1980s, with so many workers migrating to the area, I was constantly searching for someone. On this particular day, I was trying to locate an Interstate Transfer from Wyoming. He was not at the address I was given, but in checking with individuals in Hammon, I felt he was living with an Indian family at the edge of town.

It was around noon when I knocked on the front door. I was greeted by a beautiful young Indian girl who graciously invited me into the home. From the smell coming from the kitchen, I had arrived at meal time, however that did not appear to present a problem. I presented my identification, which seemed to spark the interest of two of the older children. As they bombarded me with questions about the job, the dangers, salary, benefits and other questions, an older man came into the room. He was the father of six children who were all still in the home.

I was impressed with this friendly family. They had no knowledge of the person I was searching for but offered to ask around town in an attempt to locate him. As further proof of this families hospitality, the young girl who had greeted me at the door, grabbed my hand and pulled me toward the kitchen. They insisted that I eat lunch before leaving, but as I walked into the kitchen, my appetite immediately disappeared. In the center of the table on a large blue platter was a dog. There was no mistake, it was a small dog, garnished around the edge of the platter with potatoes and carrots. I have to admit, the smell was not bad, but the vision in my head was of a small dog running around in the front yard playing with a ball. I have no idea why that popped into my head, but I knew I had to leave.

I believe the people recognized my shock at seeing their lunch as they stopped insisting I stay. As I walked toward the front door, no one said a word; the climate had changed to an embarrassing situation.

Walking across the yard to my car, I noticed a dog house and food or water bowl at the side of the residence. I tried to put it out of my mind. I never looked at a dog again in the same way, nor did I eat the rest of the day. Carrots and potatoes would never taste the same from that day on, and as I look back at that day, I don't remember eating the next day. I couldn't get the weird thoughts out of my head: did they have a cat? Where did their lunch come from? What was its name?

Time to move on.

FIREARMS INSTRUCTION AND A NINE-IRON

As I recall, my brother and I were two of the first Cleet Firearms Instructors with the Department of Corrections. We were both very active in training throughout the years.

When I worked out of District V, I was the only firearms instructor for several years. I also taught in our academy from time to time and worked with the admintration to develop guidelines and procedures relating to weapons and training. I usually enjoyed the work, although there were times when it was less than rewarding.

Under department guidelines, officers were to qualify once a year. Although we allowed some practice ammunition, it was not often that officers would fire their weapon until requalification. Some officers had difficulty qualifying. Those people would usually become a one-on-one project for me.

I had one female officer who I was working with at the Elk City Police Range. She had failed to meet firearms standards set out in our polices and procedures. After some preliminary instruction and practice firing, she began to cry, becoming so upset we stopped. She sat under a tree as she continued to cry and said she was going to lose her job. Unable to console her, I went to my vehicle, got a 9-iron and some golf balls and began chipping balls across the end of the range. I told her when she was finished, we would get back on the range.

This went on for half an hour before she got up and waved at me. She completed the course of fire with a score above 80%, which exceeded firearms standards. I told her she should be shot in the foot for putting both of us through such an ordeal, then we laughed together.

In 1989, I completed the Semi-Automatic Pistol Instructor Training, as the Department of Corrections began a transition from the revolver to the Semi-Automatic. The ordeal started all over again.

THE STING

PPCS (Pre-parole Conditional Supervision) was another of the department's "relief valve" programs to alleviate prison over-crowding. All of the early release programs were a necessary evil in an attempt to avoid over crowding, which would result in federal oversight, again.

The Department of Corrections was constantly faced with a "catch-22" situation because of increased incarcerations and lack of funds. The only way to avoid confrontation with the courts was to increase release numbers. With the public opposed to feeding the bulging monster of corrections with more and more money, and the strengthening of criminal statutes by the legislature, it was simply an impossible situation.

I was working out of the Mangum office and supervising an individual on PPCS. He was working, following the rules and reporting as instructed.

He came in one day and advised that a prison escapee had been contacting him asking for assistance. At the time, I did not have the time to deal with the situation, but when he reported the same thing the next time he came in, I listened. After checking on the escapee's record, it was apparent that he was a certain threat to the public. He did not need to remain on the streets.

My client agreed to meet the man in Oklahoma City, under the pretense of providing him with money and drugs. I advised him to remain in his vehicle when he pulled into the location in order to avoid being involved in the confrontation when the escapee arrived. He agreed.

I contacted DOC Security, arranging for a "welcoming party" when the escapee pulled into the parking lot. The next thing would be for my client to make contact and set up a date, time and location for the meeting.

Within a few days, everything was arranged. We knew what the man was driving and the fact that he would be carrying a .45 caliber pistol in his waistband. DOC Security and the Oklahoma City Police Department would be there to take the man into custody. My client would remain in his vehicle, as agreed.

Like most well laid plans, everything went wrong. The escapee did show up as arranged and was met by police and our security team, but he chose not to surrender and attempted to pull his weapon. Oklahoma City Police shot the man numerous times before he was able to get off a shot. Did I mention that my client did not stay in his vehicle as agreed? He was standing outside his car when shots were fired.

After the situation was resolved, a Detective from OCPD called me to ask what I wanted them to do with my client. I told them to take him in, interview him then release him. They agreed.

Although my PPCS client did not follow my instructions, he was instrumental in the apprehension of a dangerous escapee. I arranged relief on his sentence and fees he was required to pay.

I received an "I hope we don't have trouble over this" from my District Office, and a "Way to go Paul" from Department of Corrections Administration. I had the feeling I was working for two different agencies. I took it all in stride as I continued my philosophy of protecting the community, not following rules which could harm people.

A BOY SCOUT IN PRISON?

Exposing young men to the prison system was something I tried to do over the years. I often arranged to take a young troubled man through the prison, exposing him to what lay ahead for him if he didn't change his ways. I thought it was an effective tool in helping people make a major change in the way they were living. I had a good record until I took a Boy Scout Troop for a visit.

I contacted the warden at the Oklahoma State Reformatory, making arrangements to escort about 15 Boy Scouts through the east cell house.

At that time, the east and west cell blocks were operational, but I chose to take the scouts throught the east wing. It was usually cleaner, more open, smaller, with, usually, a somewhat better class of inmates. It was a move up for an inmate to live on the east side. The cells were four-man cells with a much larger living area. That meant more room for men to work on special projects such as leather work.

The west side, was older, not as clean, was much larger, and contained lockup, light solitary confinement and dark solitary confinement.

I lined my young Boy Scouts up before entering the rotunda, explained the general rules, plus issuance of a strict order to stay close together and away from the cells. They were a fine looking group with matching uniforms covered with patches and scout badges. I was impressed. This place would put a scare in them they wouldn't forget. Their smiling little faces took on a different look - a look of fear. This should do the trick.

We walked to the entry door leading into the cell house in a tight formation. As we walked down the run, they didn't say a word; they were too busy looking at some of the men inside the cells. Some of the inmates spoke to the young scouts as we walked by their cells. When we reached the end of the run, still in a tight group, we began our walk back. When we reached the area where we had started our tour, I asked if anyone had a question. An inmate in the second cell spoke up.

"I don't have a question, Mr. Morris, but that boy (he pointed at one of the scouts) stole a billfold out of my cell when he came by the first time."

I was appalled. A Boy Scout stealing from a prison inmate? Surely this was a mistake. "Did you take something from a cell?" I asked the young man.

He did not answer, but handed me a new billfold. I grabbed him and dragged him to the cell making him stand in front of the inmate he had stolen from. "Do you have anything you would like to say to this man?" I asked, as I returned his billfold.

"Sorry", he said.

I led my visitors out of the prison and down the front steps. When we reached the front tower, I gave them a lecture Hitler would have been proud of.

I never took another Boy Scout Troop through the prison, however, I would continue to take an individual on a tour, occasionally. I always told them about the young man who took the billfold from a cell while on a tour and described his horrifying murder only a few months later, by an escaped inmate.

There was never another theft on one of my tours.

NINETEEN (19) DUI OFFENSES

This man may hold the record for drunk driving arrests. I supervised him off and on for several years in Greer County. At one time, he was a respected electrician with a good heating and air business. But he discovered alcohol, which would cost him everything. He lost his family, his business, home, self-respect and respect from the community. He would serve countless county jail terms and at least two prison sentences. He began to mix drugs with the alcohol, began to steal, not only from family and friends, but from local businesses, who were reluctant to file charges because of his family. In spite of all these problems, he continued to operate a motor vehicle, endangering everyone he met on the road.

The local lumber yard called my office one day to advise that my client had stolen an expensive saw from their business. They did not wish to file charges, at that time; they just wanted their merchandise.

I contacted the man at his home and requested the saw. He denied taking it, but I warned him I would file charges if he didn't go get it. He pulled the item from under his bed without saying a word. I said enough for both of us.

I think everyone in the county has arrested this man at some time. DUIs were not something a Probation and Parole Officer normally dealt with, but I arrested him once when I observed him driving all over the road. I also worked for several days on one occasion, trying to locate him on an outstanding warrant. He was simply hiding from me. I found him in an abandoned house several miles north of Granite. He was drunk, sitting in a chair, listening to a portable scanner. When I found him, his comment was, "What took you so long; you must be slowing down."

Treatment did not help, jail did not help, nor did prison. He continues to drink in spite of all that has occurred in his life. It is inconceivable that an individual would continue to put themselves through a life so harmful to themselves and others.

I SEE YOUR FEET

It has often been difficult to keep a straight face because of the actions of some of the individuals I worked with. The one thing I have learned is that you should always expect the un-expected, regardless of the situation.

I had supervised an individual for several years on a sexual related offense, when he suddenly disappeared. Although he had experienced employment problems at times, he always reported regularly, followed the rules of probation and had no serious violations. None of his friends or family knew where he had gone or why he left the area. He had simply vanished.

After a couple of years, I received a telephone call from the man. He made an effort to explain why he had not reported his whereabouts for two years and finally admitted that it was wrong for him to leave without talking with me. After advising him of a warrant for his arrest, he said he would come to his parents home in Mangum the next day. He asked that I pick him up rather than have the police come to his parents home. I agreed and we set a time.

The next morning, I pulled into the driveway at his parents residence. I was invited in, offered a cup of coffee and visited briefly with the probationer and his elderly parents. We discussed his activites for the two years he was gone, before I asked if he was ready to go.

This was a man in his late 40s, in good health, with an appearance of someone who had worked out most of his life - a man's man. What he did was a complete shock to his parents and me. He ran into the bedroom next to the living room and hid under the bed. His father and I were standing beside the bed looking at his feet, which were protruding from under the bed. He was crying and shaking saying he didn't want to go to jail and that he just needed another chance. His father was standing there shaking his head with embarrassment as he scolded his son as if he were ten years old. It was a strange, and at the same time, humorous situation, however no one was laughing.

After a few minutes of scolding by his father, the man came out from under the bed, wiped the tears from his eyes and announced; "I'm ready to go."

We drove to the jail without a word. After booking him in, I went outside and had a good laugh.

I have had individuals run, jump through windows, cry and curse, throw things and resist arrest, but this was the first time I had experienced a grown man hide under his bed and wimper like a child.

You never know what a person will do when faced with confinement. When we took parole violators back to the Oklahoma State Penitentiary years ago, we watched prisoners closely as the ominous looking structure seemed to rise up out of the ground as we approached. This was a dangerous time for an officer as many would try to slip their cuffs, while others might begin to cry. It was not a great moment for anyone.

MY MOTHER-IN-LAW

I love my mother-in-law and would do most anything for her, but I didn't need her to be a reporter of criminal activity.

Several years ago, she was living alone after losing her husband to a heart attack. If you knew Jenoise, you would better understand why her neighbor was such a bother to her. She has little patience with anyone who drinks, especially to excess, or uses drugs. Her neighbor was a sloppy drunk who liked to take her clothes off and lay out on her front porch when she was drinking. This infuriated my mother-in-law. The woman was constantly coming over to her house, drunk or drinking, trying to get Jeniose to take her somewhere, loan her some money or demanding something from her.

As it would happen, my mother-in-law's neighbor was on probation for Driving Under The Influence of Alcohol and on my caseload. One morning, I received a call from Jeniose, advising her neighbor had backed her car across the street, into her yard, then began to spin the tires as she drove all the way across her lawn. She further advised that her yard was "ruined", that she wanted the woman to pay for the damage and wanted her in jail, now. I told her I would come to her house.

When I arrived at Jenoise's house, I could see the ruts across her yard; it would take some work to repair the damage. I followed the muddy tracks out into the street and on east to an intersection where she turned south. I saw her going into a mobile home about a block away. I knew she had seen me and that she would likely come back home in a few minutes. I left and drove back around where I could watch her house and waited.

I didn't wait long. I saw her walking back toward her house; I am using the term "walk" very loosely. She could barely stay on the pavement as she staggered from one side to the other. At least she was smart enough to leave her car and walk.

As she came closer, I could see that her hair was plastered against one side of her head, her clothing was filthy and wet and I could hear her cursing from a block away. When she finally saw me, she was only a few feet from her front porch, but made no effort to go home. She continued to walk toward me, striking one open hand with her fist. I could now hear her saying; "I'm gonna…….., I'm gonna…….." When she was even with my car, I opened the back door and said; "Shut up and get in." Her reply was; "Yes sir." She fell into my backseat.

LD Williams, Granite Chief of Police, arrived at about the time the woman fell into my car. LD offered to take her to jail in Mangum, so we removed her from my vehicle and put her in the patrol unit. As we drove to Mangum, she cursed both of us, beat on the security screen, threatened both of us, our families, our pets, neighbors, the neighbors relatives and pets and next of kin. She was obviously not a lady.

When we arrived at the jail, we had to force her into the booking room as she continued to spout some of the worse language I have heard coming from a woman.

This was a woman who regularly took her clothes off and climbed trees, threw things at my mother-in-law's house, turned the air blue with her foul language and was simply a nuisance. I would estimate that I have poured out five gallons of liquor in her front yard, which did little good.

She eventually left Granite. I'm not sure where she settled, but

I certainly don't miss her and I know my mother-in-law doesn't.

TAKE ME TO JAIL

It is not uncommon for a person to panic when being booked into jail. There is something about losing one's freedom that causes a person to do things they would normally not consider. That was the case in Sayre one morning.

I don't remember the young man's name or his charge, but he was being booked into jail that morning when he jumped over the front desk and was out the door before anyone could do a thing. One of the sheriff's deputies was right behind him.

I stepped outside to see what direction they were going, then I ran to my car. I drove west, as I could still see the young man and the deputy running north. Just before they were out of my sight, I saw the escapee turn west down an alley. I drove west then north down an alley in order to intercept him. I parked in the alley behind a building and peeked around a building just as the man slipped in some gravel and fell. I could not see the deputy. I just stepped back and waited for the hasty young man.

I could hear him coming and I was getting ready to stop him as he came around the building. He came around alright, but he fell again, this time losing a large patch of skin from both forearms. He simply rolled over, looked at me, then sat down on a concrete block up against a building. He just sat there bleeding, breathing heavily and shaking his head. When he got his breath, he said; "Take me to jail, please." That's what we did.

Most departments have learned to lock the front door when someone is preparing to go to jail. It saves some unnecessary running and loss of skin.

That was the only time I can remember that someone asked me to take them to jail. A novel idea.

THE DEPUTY WARDEN'S WIFE

Randolph F. Dial was convicted in Tulsa, Oklahoma for the 1981 murder of Kelly Hogan, a karate instructor; he was sentenced to a life term. Although Dial claims to have been a hit-man for the mob at the time of the murder, he was considered a pathological liar; it was difficult to separate the truth from fiction. He was born in Tulsa, Oklahoma in 1944, was an artist and sculptor with a checkered past. Married at least three times and divorced three times, he had three children.

Dial transferred to the Oklahoma State Reformatory, obtained trustee status then began working on pottery projects in the garage of the Deputy Warden, Randy Parker. Bobbie Parker, wife of Randy Parker, was overseeing his work, until both disappeared from the reformatory grounds August 30, 1994. According to investigative reports, authorities felt Dial kidnapped Mrs. Parker.

Parker left her husband and two daughters, ages ten and eight behind on that day. Bobbie was very close to her family, leaving investigators convinced that she would not have gone with Dial willingly. Although she made a couple of telephone calls following her disappearance, the trail grew cold, with no further contact with her.

I think every officer in the area was out the night Dial and Parker disappeared. I was notified as soon as authorties learned of the incident and started a search of the area around Quartz Mountain Park. I had not paired with another officer, but, continued to search the area around the park.

I was crossing the railroad tracks on my way out of the park when my lights picked up a reflection of tail lights on a dirt road to the north. I backed up and was pulling in behind what appeared to be a van, about the same color as the vehicle Parker was driving when kidnapped. The vehicle's lights suddenly came to life as the driver began spinning the tires as the vehicle sped north. The dust from the vehicle was very thick making the visibility less than twenty-five feet, which caused me to slow my vehicle. It was then, however, that I realized the road we were on was a dead end, ending at the foot of the dam less than a mile ahead. I tried to stay as close to the vehicle as possible to avoid losing the driver if he decided to abandon the vehicle.

It seemed like only a few seconds before we were making a slight turn toward the dam. The dust was not as bad as I watched the vehicle slow, pull up on a slight rise at the foot of the dam, and stop.

I should have checked in with Mangum Police Department during the short chase, but I was busy retrieving my shotgun from the backseat. I certainly didn't intend to lose this short run, as I felt I had Mr. Dial.

Just as I stepped out of my vehicle, I saw the dome light come on in the vehicle as a young man, with his girlfriend by his side, began to dig through his billfold for his driver's license. I had captured a couple of kids, necking. Brilliant.

I put my shotgun back in the vehicle and walked up to the side of the vehicle, which, by the way, turned out to be a full sized car, not a van. It was, however, the correct color.

The young man handed me his driver's license.

"Why did you run from me?" I asked.

"I was afraid of getting a ticket, sir."

I explained the situation to the couple, telling them the vehicle was the same color as the suspected escapee was driving, although it was not a van. I told them to get off the roads. Then I went home.

Dial and Parker would remain on the run for the next eleven years. Although her husband never gave up hope that she would some day come home, her two girls practically grew up without a mother.

In April, 2005, after America's Most Wanted received a tip, Dial and Parker were located in Shelby County Texas, working on a chicken farm. They were living in a two-bedroom mobile home in an isolated area of the county. Dial offered no resistance when arrested at the trailer after Bobbie had been picked up at her jobsite. He did have a pistol in the residence at the time of his arrest. It was reported that they had worked at the chicken farm for the past five and one-half years. Dial had been fired by the chicken ranch, but had pressured Bobbie to take on extra work to make up for him not working. After Dial's arrest, he indicated his relationship with Parker was never a romantic one. He claimed to have made threats against her children if she did not cooperate and remain with him. He continued to tell authorities that he kidnapped Parker at knife point, telling her he would harm her children if she attempted to escape. He said their relationship was similar to the "Stockholm Syndrome" in which hostages sometimes become sympathetic with their captors.

Randy and Bobbie Parker were reunited and no charges were filed immediately against her. Dial was charged with Escape From a Penal Institution in Greer County, but did not answer questions regarding his escape and kidnapping of Parker. He was returned to prison to serve the remainder of his life sentence and the seven year escape sentence.

Dial died of unknown causes June 13, 2007, while serving his prison term at the Oklahoma State Penitentiary.

Randolph Dial was a con-man, master manipulator and vain individual. I doubt that he knew the difference between the truth and a lie, as his life was built on deception. In a letter written by Dial to the New York Times, he said while he and Parker were together, she was kidnapped by a pair of Louisiana swamp rats, whom he had to kill in order to rescue her.

Dial created his own world. He created his own tales to make himself appear as some sort of hero, when in actuality, he was no more than a common criminal, guilty of serious crimes against humanity. I doubt that he will be missed.

Within the past few weeks, the Greer County District Attorney's Office in Mangum, Oklahoma announced the filing of formal felony charges against Bobbie Parker. After a three year investigation by the Oklahoma State Bureau of Investigation, and only days before the statute of limitation expired in the case, the District Attorney has advised that the state has credible information that Bobbie Parker aided Dial in the escape and the two were romantically involved. A trial date has not been set. The saga continues.

DISTRICT IV

Transferring to District IV was the most difficult decision I had ever made, while working with the Department Of Corrections. I had been in District V my entire career, had trained many of the people and supervised many of them over the years. They were like my own family.

I was considering early retirement, but needed to increase my salary level to raise my retirement. I had supervised personnel before when Officer II was established, but I never enjoyed the work. But, I had to think about my level of income and retirement funds.

There was an opening for a Team Supervisor in District IV, Altus, Oklahoma. As the distance was only twenty-five miles from my home in Granite, I felt this would be my last opportunity to advance without leaving the area. With my mother-in-law's health and her need for assistance, it would have been impossible for us to re-locate. I applied for the position and was accepted.

In 1997, I began working in District IV as Team Supervisor for the Altus area. I was responsible for ten Officers and a clerk scattered over six counties and six offices. In addition to that work, the District Supervisor, Wayne Smith, asked that I act as Assistant District Supervisor out of Lawton Office until the job could filled. I was not interested in the position because of my family and the fact that I only wished to work three years. It was an interesting but exhausting undertaking.

I recall one of first days in Lawton as the assistant. There were attorneys waiting to talk with me regarding weapons confiscated from their clients by my officers. I couldn't believe an attorney (I assume had passed the bar) was asking that I give handguns back to their clients who were felons. I asked that their request be repeated, thinking perhaps I had misunderstood. I heard correctly. I just ran them out of my office.

Although I was running all the time, I developed a great deal of respect for District IV Officers and staff. They were hard-working, dedicated individuals much like the people I had left in District V.

In the Altus office, Karen Dudash, Doug Abbott and Dale Landers were the officers working Jackson County and Frederick. They were all good officers. Karen was always willing to help with any project. Her casework was some of the best in the District. Dale Landers was one of the best field officers I had. I could depend on Dale for anything.

Harlan Ross worked the Washita County area. He and I had worked together before, in District V. Harlan always knew his clients and their families very well. He acting and dressed in a very professional manner. Because of his experience, he had a great deal of respect from the officials in his county.

Eugene Hopper was in the Mangum office, working Greer County and Harmon County. Eugene's knowledge of the law, department procedures and policies, his relationships with law enforcement, court officials and other departments and agencies, were invaluable. He was always willing to do, with professionalism, whatever was asked of him. He also had a great deal of respect in the area he worked. I can't say much about his driving, however.

Susan Tedford was the officer in Hobart. Susan was a good officer, but began to burn out during the time I supervised her. I knew she would quit at some point, but tried to keep her with us. After I retired, she took a position with an institution.

The Anadarko office was always a bright spot in my day. Although the driving distance was greater than I desired, I always enjoyed visiting with the officers there; Jeff Woody, Brian Thornburgh and Tess Brown. They required very little supervision. Their cases were always up to date and correct, with little difficulty performing their jobs. They were some of the best officers I had ever worked with.

The Frederick office was filled by Denese Due, a former police office in Frederick. Denese was a knowlegable officer, worked hard and had no problems with the job. Her experience as a police officer was a great asset.

Beatrice Sands, my clerk and friend. She was always on top of everything regardless of the work load. She was my calendar, my advisor, go-between from my office to the court, detective and deputy. If she had not been there, I don't know that I could have finished the three years with District IV. When my Mother was in the hospital, she was there; when I didn't have time to check on her, she was there. I can't say enough about Beatrice.

BABY OIL

Dale Landers came to us from the Oklahoma State Reformatory where he worked as a correctional officer. He completed CLEET with high scores in marksmanship, and would go on to make an outstanding field officer.

A women in Frederick, who had mental problems, was apparently off her medication one day, when several calls came into the Frederick Police Department. She was also on Dale's caseload, and he responded with police to the calls from citizens.

The women was walking down the street in Frederick, with no clothes, plus she had rubbed herself down with baby oil. She was throwing rocks, turning over swing sets and anything else she could topple over. She was clearly out of control.

Dale and other officers, got more than they bargained for. They ran her around a few yards, but could not hold her because of the baby oil. They rolled her around in the dry grass trying to restrain her, but could not. I think they finally ran her into an open storm shelter and drove one of their cars up on the door.

They were all covered with baby oil and dry grass when they returned to the office.

I only wish I could have seen it.

BEWARE OF THE DRUNK INDIANS

No, I have nothing at all against Indians. But, in the Carnegie and Anadarko area, you occasionally run across one of them on the road, driving drunk.

When I was farming, my brother and I would often get behind

at peanut harvest, and call for trucks out of Carnegie. Usually, the loaders and stackers were Indians hired by the Gold Kist Company to load and haul sacked, dried peanuts back to the warehouses in Caddo County. They were excellent stackers, but always did a better job with additional whiskey, which they always carried with them. I remember one year, they set our pasture on fire when they built a small fire in order to warm. Before they would leave our fields, most of them were drunk, but their stack jobs were perfect.

If only the alcohol had the same effect with their driving as with their ability to stack peanut sacks.

I was coming back from Anadarko in the afternoon when I saw a pickup just ahead of me. It was running vehicles off the road. I pulled closer to the vehicle and noticed the driver was having difficulty sitting upright. He was weaving back and forth as he drove from ditch to ditch. Vehicles meeting him were pulling off the roadway to avoid a head-on collision.

After he ran several cars off the road, with one of them a close call, I decided I needed to get him off the road. I was getting closer to him when we topped a hill where there was a wide intersection and a closed convenience store. He pulled off the roadway, stopped and passed out. I got out and removed his keys from the ignition, made sure he was alright and called for assistance. The Oklahoma Highway Patrol picked up my transmission at about the same time a BIA Officer answered. He drove up within a few minutes. We pulled the guy out of the vehicle, checked his ID and waited for OHP. When they arrived, we loaded him in their unit and all went home.

These are the types of people who wipe out entire families on the highways. I have pulled people out of vehicles that were hit by drunk drivers - some were dead. Because of some of the things I have seen on the highways, I have no sympathy for a drunk driver.

ENGLAND

In May, 1999, we took the trip of a life-time. With Peggy and George Roach, we flew to England where we stayed for two weeks, touring the country.

We initially flew out of Will Rogers Airport in Oklahoma City to Dallas where we would take British Air to England.

I remember flying out of Will Rogers and tracing the path of a violent tornado that struck the area only two weeks before. The path of the monster F5 tornado was very clear. The grass had been pulled out of the ground leaving a reddish/brown path dotted by cement foundations where homes previously stood. The path reminded me of a lazy river flowing leisurely through the country side. But, there was nothing pleasant about the sight; 44 people lost their lives during that violent storm with more than 700 injuries reported.

The outbreak of tornadoes that day, was the largest ever reported in the state of Oklahoma, with a financial loss estimated at 1.3 billion dollars. Sixty-one (61) tornados were reported that day; it was the most ever reported in Oklahoma's history. Sixteen (16) counties were declared disaster areas.

Landing in Dallas, we had to hurry in order to catch our flight with British Air. Linda and I had been on several commercial flights, but never the quality or pleasant reception as received with British Air. The seats were spacious with televisions in the back of each seat. We were fortunate that we were allowed to walk around, visit with other passengers, or sit near the front and watch the ocean pass underneath. It was the most pleasant flight I had been on, even though it was around 11 hours in duration. I didn't particularly care for all the water as far as a person could see, but you can't live forever.

We flew into Gatwick Airport, the second largest airport in Britain after Heathrow. Gatwick has the longest single runway of any airport in the world, with direct connections to Victoria Station, officially known as London Victoria.

Coming from a law enforcement background, I have always been interested in other country's public safety systems, particularly England. Knowing that most officers in England do not carry firearms, I was surprised when the first officer I saw as I came off the plane, was carrying an Uzi, a fully automatic weapon slung over his shoulder. I'm sure the tight security is a necessity, considering the international traffic coming through Gatwick.

Once through customs, we went directly to the light rail and took it into Victoria Station in Westminster, one of the busiest places in the world. Simply watching the different groups of people coming and going through the concourse, was amazing. I was stunned by the architecture and the fact that they seldom tear a building down; they repair. Unlike Americans, who level a building and build another, they seem to be more conservative when it comes to building.

Being unfamiliar with the surroundings, we got into a line of people waiting for a taxi. At least, we thought we in the line. What we had done, was walk to what we thought was the end, but the line actually continued on the other side of the street. A rather large, but friendly, man approached us and advised we were "bucking the queue." We had to think a moment to know what he was saying, then we apologized and went to the end of the "correct" line. He was telling us we had gone ahead of the other people in line who were waiting across the street. At least he was very polite. In the United States, someone would have probably punched one of us, or at a minimum, lashed out with obscene language or other strange actions.

Then came our taxi ride into London. That was an experience in itself, somewhat different from driving in the states. I tried to watch the driver as much as possible as I knew we would be driving, at some time. The absence of collisions in London, speaks volumes for the drivers there. Driving often without street markings, and only inches apart, was amazing. It is nothing like the traffic we have in our larger cities. The British seldom honk, make obscene gestures or curse each other. In fact, they are extremely courteous.

The round-a-bouts were something new. Instead of stop lights, the British have round-a-bouts, which are intersections, but built in circular patterns with several different roads branching off in different directions. They are very efficient, in my opinion, much more so than stop lights. As a person enters the round-a-bout, he locates the road he wishes to take and simply takes that road from the circle. No vehicles stop and waste fuel. We could learn something from their road builders, but they do continue to drive on the wrong side of the road.

Within a few minutes, we were in front of the "flat" where we would be staying with George's step-sister and her husband, Jim and Rita Gunter. She was employed by Kerr McGee as an administrator with the European section of the company. I never understood what her position was with the company, but she and her husband were gracious hosts. The "flat" was in the high-rent district of London. At one time, the Beatles lived just across the street.

We remained in London for several days, riding the excellent transportation system, seeing as many things as possible. The British are masters at maintaining transportation sources for their citizens. We purchased tickets for the "tubes" which were also used for bus transportation. With the color-coded mapping system, it was simple to go wherever we wanted, with little assistance.

I initially had problems with the currency, especially the "pound coin" which was almost a quarter-inch thick and the size of a nickel. A person could not carry many of them without being uncomfortable. After simply holding my hand out with money covering my palm and letting a merchant make change, I soon learned the monetary system.

Peggy is one of the funniest people I have ever known. A Joan Rivers clone, she is a person of genuineness, and honesty, with a love for cruises and chocolate. She also has the ability to make me lose my breath when making one of her confusing statements. For example: "Strike while you have the bird in the hand."

When we were still on the farm, she wanted to know why each cow didn't have her own bull. I think I told her I couldn't afford that many bulls.

While we were traveling in England, Scotland and Wales, we would often lose her while we were eating, then find her in the kitchen where she would be getting recipes from the chefs. She is a pleasure to be around. She has even influenced Linda with her statements. A few days ago, Linda said, "That's just bridge under the water." It's obvious, they are cousins.

We stayed a short walk from Hyde Park, known for public speeches at the north-east corner of the park. Known as Speaker's Corner, it is a location set aside for public speakers to make their positions on any issue available to those listening. People are allowed to talk with no time limits, as long as there is no profane language or disturbances. We also learned that other Speaker's Corners were located at Kennington Park, Finsbury Park and Victoria Park.

We watched as a fairly large number of Bobbies were going to the Hyde Park area, one morning. We decided to go along, however, we left our wives behind, in case there were problems. By the number of police, we expected something. I think, normally, the authorities are relatively tolerant with speakers, but will not tolerate disturbances.

That morning, I never understood what one of the speakers was promoting as he shouted and yelled in Arabic, but he had collected more than his share of hecklers. The shouting became louder and louder until officers hauled several away.

We had seen and heard enough.

We were ready to leave London on our whirlwind trip. A vehicle was reserved at Victoria for seven days, but when we unloaded our luggage at the car rental, they told us they had no more automatics. The only vehicle available was a Rover, 4-cylinder, 5-speed standard shift, hatchback. George and I just stared at the small, blue car, wondering if we could get all our luggage in the back, or leave one of the wives. We decided to give it a try, loaded our bags, pulled out of Victoria Station and were immediately lost. I was driving (trying to drive) with no earthly idea which direction to go, but the immediate problem was not only staying on the wrong side of the street, but mastering a vehicle made for the dyslexic. Everything was backward; my passenger was on the wrong side; I was on the wrong side, as well as the steering wheel, and instruments. It would take some time to overcome my Yankee driving skills.

Our plans were to get on the motorway, travel north toward Scotland, driving until almost night then find a bed and breakfast in the country. I had followed someone who appeared to be going to the motorway, luckily getting something right. Once we were on the motorway, I learned to drive.

Although we stayed lost most of time (which was another part of the adventure) things were going well. I had not killed anyone, although I did run one driver off the road and scared another half-to-death when I reverted back to the right side of the road. Everything considered, and the fact that we were all in one piece, I felt I had mastered the left-handed car. The only serious problem I encountered was the round-a-bouts. After several circles around the "rolling intersection" I conquered the concept, in spite of my back-seat drivers. Everyone had a different idea where we should go and when to turn. I became a deaf mute for several hundred miles, only listening to my official navigator, George.

Other than Heaven, the most beautiful place I would ever hope to see, was one of our first stops - Chatsworth, the home of the Duke and Duchess of Devonshire. Probably older than anything I had ever seen, Chatsworth and its grounds appeared to have been manicured by God Himself. The rolling hills were covered by a dark, green and healthy grass resembling carpet - all the same height.

Leaving Chatsworth, we began searching for a bed and breakfast in the area, with little time remaining before the sunset. We were fortunate to see a small sign, partially covered by weeds, with directions to the Temperance House Farm, a farm and bed and breakfast a short distance from Chatsworth. This would prove to be one of the highlights of our adventure in England.

Angela Dethick, her husband, children and the grandfather, owned and operated the beautiful old Temperance Inn, near Chesterfield, Derbyshire. The Inn had been converted to a bed and breakfast, but was an active farm with several head of cattle enjoying belly-high grass. They actually appeared to be overly fat, but probably just healthy livestock.

The history and background of the property was truly fascinating, as explained by Dethick's grandfather. Almost blind, the old gentleman loved his history, especially the history of the Temperance Inn. At one time, the Inn was a pub and hotspot in the area, but patrons would over-indulge then go to the grounds at Chatsworth where they helped themselves to hares. When the thefts were discovered and traced back to the Temperance Inn, the place was shut down by authorities.

The property had been in the family for years, but Angela and her husband, needing the extra income, opened the bed and breakfast. They were wonderful people, not like most bed and breakfast hosts who would prepare patron's meals then leave; the Dethicks would sit down with us and share a meal. They became as our own family, hugging us when we had to leave.

Although I can't recall all the places we visited, I remember the Old Mause Bed and Breakfast near Lockerbie, Scotland. Of course, Lockerbie was the site of the Pan Am Flight 103 bombing December 21, 1988, when the commercial airline exploded over Lockerbie. The town still bears the scars from the horrific explosion and the raining down of metal, fuel and body parts on the town. Lockerbie residents still talk about what took place there almost twenty years ago. The loss of 259 lives would brand this small city forever. It would take more than 11 years to bring those responsible to justice, because the country of Libya and their leader, Kaddafi, refused to extradite the murderers. After a lengthy investigation and agreement with Kaddafi, one of the men was convicted and sentenced to life in prison. The other suspect was acquitted and released.

We drove through Wales, spending the night at a small motel situated on the coast near enough to the ocean to watch ships cross on the horizon. I remember the fun we had when we saw letters on the pavement we thought meant something about dogs or livestock. We later learned the markings were alerting us to slow down. I suppose we should research a countries language before trying to drive across the land.

One of the lighter moments was at a place we stayed in Rapon. Early in the morning, Linda and I heard a horrible crash in the bathroom we shared with George and Peggy. George was taking a shower when he slipped and fell, taking the shower surround down with him. He fell out of the tub lodging between the tub and the wall. When I opened the bathroom door, the place resembled something that was being demolished in order to rebuild. He was not hurt, and within a short time, we had repaired the shower enclosure. We have not allowed him to forget it.

On our way back into London, we traveled through the lake district stopping at some of the more beautiful places.

Coming into London, after a 1400 mile journey across England, Scotland and Wales, I felt like one of the taxi drivers. Traveling on the wrong side of the road did not seem so bad.

Truly a trip of a lifetime; I hope someday to return to England.

MOTHER

On November 24, 1999, I lost my Mother to a heart attack. Her heart simply gave out on her.   She was 84 when she passed away at the Jackson County Memorial Hospital, Altus, Oklahoma.

I had just visited with her that afternoon, but she told me not to worry. She said she knew she wasn't going to live long, but did not want me to worry if something happened. Of course I didn't want to hear that, and simply tried to tell her she would be fine in a few days. I also knew her health was very bad.

Her death was very hard for me to accept. I don't know if it was because I had lost my Father and she was my only parent, or if it was the fact that she was my Mother. She and I were always close, as was my father. It was just very difficult. I don't think anyone can prepare for a loved one's death, even if you know they are going to die. It is always a shock.

My brother and I had tried to keep her at home as long as possible, because she was happier there. We stayed with her many nights and days, taking turns as she needed us. Because I was still working, by brother probably spent more time with her as he was retired, but it was a difficult time for all of us.

I miss my parents very much, but I would not wish them back

to this earth with the health problems both of them endured. I know they are both in a better place. I look forward to seeing them someday.

RETIREMENT

The day I had waited for - retirement. Although ready to end the "rat race," I also began to experience mixed emotions about leaving the many people I had worked with so many years. More than 30 years of going to work each day, answering the phone in the middle of the night, worrying about my officers, and the chase. I would miss receiving the longevity award at state meetings when the speaker would ask, "Is Morris here?" But, more than anything, I would miss the friends I had made over the years while on the job. I knew it would be difficult.

Perhaps I could have used a different word than "chase", but locating absconders, escapees, individuals who were wanted - those were the aspects of the work I enjoyed and would miss. I prided myself in my ability to track people, regardless of the circumstances. It was not only the result of good training, but the things taught me by my Father. I knew I would miss all of those things.

I would also miss being on the firing range and in the classroom instructing new officers in weapon safety and use. Although I would remain a Cleet Firearms Instructor after retirement, I would no longer have the contact with officers that I enjoyed so much.

I would no longer worry about Harlan smoking in his state vehicle, Eugene putting someone in the hospital or some idiot calling my home when I was gone and cursing at my wife. But there was the other side of the coin. I would no longer be called in the middle of the night, struggle to meet some survey that was due yesterday, discipline an officer or talk with attorneys who seldom understood what we were all about and didn't care. I would no longer wake up in the middle of the night in a cold sweat because I dreamed I had failed to complete a mandatory form.

Linda and I would have the freedom to visit our daughters

anytime we wanted or load the Harley down for a two or three- day cruise to who-knows-where. I could sleep as long as I wanted without worrying about a phone call or police knocking at my door. The only thing I had to worry about would be the "honey-do list" Linda had been working on for more than 30 years. Mixed emotions again.

The retirement party in Lawton was very nice. I received praise I probably didn't deserve, plaques, my badge and some stories detailing some of the dumber things I had done throughout the years (those came from Eugene). That didn't bother me in the least because I knew he would be retiring before long.

After the get-together, Linda and I returned home, but I had one more job to complete. I think it was around 8:00 or 9:00 that evening when Officer Susan Davis telephoned to advise of a methamphetamine lab at one of her parolee's mobile home in Snyder, Oklahoma. She said she had some police officers with her, but needed permission to kick the door in because he would not respond.

I called District IV Supervisor Wayne Smith. After explaining the situation, he authorized the action, but requested I go to the scene and supervise the entry. I went to the closet and began putting my gear on; ballistic vest, cuffs, weapon, etc. Linda came into the room and wanted to know what I thought I was doing as I had just retired. The explanation was not sufficient as she began to cry and begged me not to go. In all the years I worked, she never requested me not to go into a situation of this nature. Her explanation was that I was retired and it would be our lack of luck that I would be killed the last day of my job.

I took everything off, putting it back in the closet, then I started to telephone some of my other officers to assist Susan. I called Wayne and told him the situation at home, but he asked that I just show up in Snyder, stand back out of the way and merely oversee what was done. Although Linda still didn't approve, she would agree as long as I promised not to get involved.

I put everything back on and left for Hobart to pick up a state vehicle then to Snyder. I called Susan and advised her I would be at her location as soon as possible, but before I could get through Lone Wolf, I was stopped by their officer for speeding, and I was definitely speeding. As I got out of my vehicle, the officer made this comment, "Well, what do we have here?" My answer was, "What you have is a man in a hurry to get to Snyder to assist with a methamphetamine lab." I just got back in my vehicle and drove off. I thought he could get me when I came back through.

Once I had picked up the state vehicle, I drove to Snyder where Susan and other officers were waiting. She had found a methamphetamine solution settling out in quart jars on wooden shelves outside the man's home. Her attempts to get the man to the door had failed, although she had made numerous attempts. We could hear conversations of some sort, coming from inside the trailer.

My officers had already discussed my involvement in going into the residence. They asked me not to come near the front door, that they would make the entry not taking a chance on me getting hurt. They kicked the door, entered the residence, but did not find the owner, only 2 police scanners, one at each end of the trailer. Officers did confiscate about a dozen firearms from the mobile home while the Jackson County Drug Task Force confiscated the illegal drugs and paraphernalia. I advised Susan to label, check serial numbers and store the weapons at the Kiowa County Sheriff's Department and file charges on the individual the next morning in the county and request a DOC Warrant.

I think I returned home at around 5:30 in the morning, topping off my career with a few extra hours I wouldn't be paid for, but what else is new?

FROM RETIREMENT TO WORK

I remember the feeling I had the morning after I retired. I didn't realize how much stress I was under all those years until I opened my eyes that morning with plans for the day running through my mind. Then, the pleasant but jolting shock; I don't have to make plans; I'm retired. I have never had such a wonderful feeling.

Our best friends and travel buddies, George and Peggy Roach live in an old two-story house in Mangum, built in the early 1900s. After I retired, we decided to remodel the upstairs, build a walk-in closet and completely re-build the upstairs bathroom. We cut out part of the old attic, installed a Jacuzzi tub and built a shower.

Because of the age of the house, most of the wood was so hard, we had to drill holes before driving a nail. During the time when this house was originally built, the dimensions of lumber was different than now. A 2 x 4 today, measures approximately 3 1/2 " x 1 ¾", much different from the actual 2" x 4" measurements of one-hundred years ago.

The only real memorable moment we had while working on the house, was when I became lodged in a small crawl space while plumbing the Jacuzzi. George had to take the fireplace out of the bedroom in order to pull me out, feet first. We all had a good laugh.

Shortly after remodeling George and Peggy Roach's house, we started on my home. George and I dug a brick ledge footing, set the molding at the top, and made other preparations to brick the house. We put in new windows, a set of French doors leading out of the living room onto the deck, and I dug Linda a fish pond. I don't know what I was thinking.

The house was bricked by a man and his son from Altus using tumbled, red brick from the Mangum Brick Plant. Following Linda's retirement and the closing of her beauty shop, which was located between the kitchen and the garage, we tiled the floor in that room and turned it into an office. After our house project was completed, Linda and I began helping her brother - who purchased a house next door to us - remodel his home. We completed that job in approximately three months.

The next project was to re-build a small house for my mother-in-law. Her health was preventing her from caring for the large home she owned in east Granite, so she sold it and purchased a smaller home only four blocks from Linda and me. Doc (Linda's brother) and I worked on the house for several weeks. We replaced the cabinets, floor covering and major appliances before she moved in. The roof was also replaced.

George and I later built a ceramic shower for his daughter and her husband, Mickey and Georganna Lively, in Mangum, before we retired again, hopefully from rebuilding.

I was also working part-time for CA Warren, helping him farm in the Brinkman area. I worked for CA about five years running tractors, fencing, spraying, feeding cattle and many other farm related jobs. I enjoyed the work and the time I spent with my good friend who I had gone to school and graduated with. When we were tired of working, we would go to the golf course, usually playing with Jerry McGavock, Bill Davis and Glen (Guinea) Sewell. We had some great times.

Dan Deaver, who was a good friend, stopped in my driveway one afternoon with a big request. Dan was born and grew up in the Mangum area. He later worked as an ATF Agent until retiring and completing law school. He completed his studies, passed the bar and was working as an Assistant District Attorney in Greer County.

I had told Dan, several years before, I would help him if he ever decided to run for Associate District Judge in Greer County. I had almost forgot the promise I made to him, but he had not. Dan asked that I be his campaign manager for the race for Associate District Judge. How could I possibly refuse. So, for the next few months, Linda and I, along with several other supporters, went to work to put Dan in office. Things went very well. Dan won the election by a great number of votes. He is still the Associate District Judge in Greer County. Thus far, he has not drawn an opponent.

ENJOYING RETIREMENT

Since retirement, Linda and I have enjoyed two cruises with George and Peggy Roach. I have never enjoyed anything as I have the opportunity to cruise the Caribbean with good friends, watching great musical productions and shopping, but mostly, eating.

There is something about being on a ship almost as large as the town we live in, watching the ocean and the occasional dolphin along side, that simply calmed my soul. It is the most relaxing vacation I have had.

If you want to seriously relax and leave your troubles behind, book a cruise. The cost is about a 100.00 a day, with someone to make your bed, bring food to your cabin and make strange towel art. I am checking into the cost of living on a ship compared to a nursing home. The ship may be cheaper. Check it out.

Shortly after I retired, I purchased a 1997 Harley Davidson Sportster motorcycle, something I had always wanted. I had never got the "Cushman" motor scooter out of my blood.

Linda and I started riding, often with friends who also enjoyed the fresh air and wide open spaces. But before long, we were wanting a cruiser, with plans to travel across country with friends. I started searching for a larger bike. From a newspaper article in Altus, Oklahoma, I located my dream ride - a 2001 Harley Davidson Road King, black with over $3000.00 in chrome and extras. It had less that 6000 miles on the odometer. I bought it, with Linda's blessings.

There is something about riding a motorcycle that a person can't experience any other way. The freedom a person feels, the smells and the wind blowing across your body; it is hard to describe. For me, troubles and concerns I might have, disappear from the seat of my Harley. It is simply a wonderful feeling.

Although we have traveled to some extent, it has been difficult to make the trips we have planned. Linda was diagnosed with colon cancer in 2004, which altered our plans for a time. But her surgery was successful. We were very fortunate in that the cancer was small and had not breached the wall of the colon. She was not required to have any other treatment. We were very blessed and thankful for all the prayers, which I believe, were significant in her overcoming cancer.

We are again, making plans to travel across country on the

Road King. But I must tell you about the ride with several of my friends just last year. It was the most memorable trip I can remember.

George Roach, Dr. Phillip Kingery, his son David, his friend Jeff Merrell and I, decided to ride across Oklahoma to Mena, Arkansas. The trip would take us across eastern Oklahoma, over the Talimena Scenic Drive then into Arkansas. Talimena Drive is 54 miles of winding roads that crosses the top of the Ouachita Mountains in the far eastern area of Oklahoma. It is known for its spectacular autumn color, brought to life during the fall as the foliage reacts to colder weather. It is one of the most beautiful places in Oklahoma.

Phillip, George and I, rode to Ada, where we met David and Jeff. We then traveled on across the state, enjoying frequent breaks, enjoyable conversation and the countryside. As I said, there is not a feeling like riding.

Our stop in McAlester would be a memorable one. We all pulled into a convenience store on the east side of town, were filling up with fuel and stretching our legs, when we saw a tall black man walking toward us. He was coming from the east, walking along the sidewalk, talking or singing to himself, stomping his feet and swinging his arms. I had the feeling he had mental problems, from the way he acted. He seemed to focus on us as he continued to walk our way, stomping his feet, jiving and singing. Although I was carrying a handgun, I didn't feel threatened enough to draw it. Instead, I reached into by roll bag, removed a lock blade knife, opened it and held it at my side. I think the man saw the knife, because he stopped, stared, made a few facial adjustments, then walked over to an air hose about 15 yards from us. The air hose, coiled around an old tire rim that hung on a steel post and had an air chuck at the end. Our black admirer walked over to the air hose, pulled about a foot of it from the rim and stuck it in his right ear. As if talking on a telephone, he said, in a loud voice, "You know that white trash up on the hill? Well, it's back again." He placed the air hose back on the tire rim and walked on. It was the funniest thing I had seen in years.

After we had all laughed for about ten minutes, we managed to get back on the road. Every few miles for the hour, I broke out in laughter that would almost cause me to pull over. I could also see the other guys doing the same thing. If I had only taken a photo.

We arrived at the beginning of Talimena Drive, with plenty of time to ride across and into Mena before the sun set. The ride was spectacular. The winding road, the slight breeze through the tall pines and the aromas as we rode across the mountain were wonderful, until we had reached the top. I was behind Jeff, who was following Phillip as we came upon some tight curves. I had just started around one the curves, when I suddenly saw a windshield flying through the air, and Phillips legs, also flying through the air. Phillip's bike was on its side about five feet off the pavement, the windshield was a few feet away and he was now on his feet trying to lift the bike. We had all stopped and were trying to determine if he was injured. We were very fortunate. He had tried to make the curve a little fast, ran off the pavement into the damp grass which caused the motorcycle to lose traction and slip out from under him. The important thing was, he was not hurt. The Harley, however, did have problems; the shifting lever had sheared off. We managed to get the bike in a lower gear and headed toward Mena, Arkansas. Unable to go more than 40 or 50 mph, it took us somewhat longer, but we still arrived at a motel in Mena before sundown.

After having an enjoyable dinner at a local restaurant and learning from our young waiter that Mena was actually a drug drop from Columbia, we returned to the motel to work on Phillip's bike. I borrowed a couple of hammers from the motel owner and George and I (the MacGyvers of the bunch) were able to drive the shifter back on the transmission shaft. We didn't know if it would hold, but it was on.

We were exhausted. George and I stayed in a room together - if you could call it a room - with the strangest shower I had seen. The shower head was even with my chest and when the water was turned on, it came out of everything in the bathroom. I had to bend over to take a shower; I don't know how George managed, being six foot tall. But, the bed's were good.

The next morning, we were off. I pulled over in Talihina, bought a couple of tubes of JB Weld Quickset, then ran the guys down. While we stopped for a few minutes, I applied the JB Weld, put tape over it so it would stay in place, and waited for a few minutes for it to harden. The Harley may wear out, but the JB Weld will still be there.

I don't know when I have enjoyed anything more than riding across the country with friends. As George Eliot said:

> "Friendship is the inexpressible comfort
> Of feeling safe with a person, having
> Neither to weigh thoughts nor measure
> Words."

FAMILY

I have done many things in my life, but most have been approached with my wife and children foremost in my mind. They are my inspiration and reason for penning these words to paper.

I have had several opportunities to advance within the Department of Corrections, but most would have involved moving my family. I wanted both my daughters, Shannon and Sharra, to finish high school in a small school, preferably, Granite Public School. As a result, I remained a field officer for most of my career, only accepting a supervisor's position my last three years and after my daughters were out of school. I have never regretted my decision.

Shannon (Morris) Wood has been married ten years to a wonderful young man (Chris) who is like my own son. Shannon is a wonderful mother and wife with a unfailing outlook on life. She is a college graduate with a Masters Degree. I have always been very proud of her and love her very much.

Although Chris was born and reared in Pennsylvania where people have never learned to speak English, he attended and graduated from the Oklahoma University at Norman, Oklahoma, gradually building his "Okie" vocabulary to an acceptable level. He is now able to say words such as, "shoot yea", big-ole", "fixin ta", "I'm gonna do it", "wer levin now," and "whut cha doin?" I knew with a little prodding and good examples, he would finally come around to a proper way of speaking. I don't think Shannon could have married a better man.

My two red-headed Grandsons are a blessing in my life and one of the reasons I am still living. Connor, who is six now, and Nathan three, are making their parents pay for the way they lived. They are very special little young men with big hearts, full of love and a fraction of mischief, as it should be. I love them very much, but as they live in Denver, Colorado, Linda and I do not see them as much as we would like, although the time we spend with them is quality.

My youngest daughter, Sharra, has been a special person in my life from the time I held her in my arms when she was a tiny baby. A good athlete, Valedictorian of her graduating class, an honest, caring person who I love very much. Sharra is a college graduate with two Master Degrees and works with abused children. We are fortunate in that Sharra lives only three hours from us, making visiting less of a problem.

MY CLOSEST CALL

I have always heard about people retiring then dying. I suppose I can almost put myself in that category.

I had been retired for about six years when the world suddenly stopped and tried to kick me off. I was working in the yard, shredding small limbs in a chipper-shredder, when I began experiencing chest pains. I had felt these pressure sensations before, but thought they were a result of my shoulder injury. I had pulled my left shoulder out of place a few years before while wrestling with a jail escapee. The pains had always gone away as I held my arms up over my head. Because of the subsiding pain, I felt it was the shoulder.

I sat on the tailgate of my truck, raised my arms, but this time, the pain did not go away. Linda probably saved my life by stuffing two aspirins down my throat and demanding that we call an ambulance. I still refused to believe I was having a heart attack, but agreed to let her drive me to the hospital as opposed to an ambulance.

When we arrived at the Mangum City Hospital, they immediately began treating me for a heart attack. After several tests, nitro drip and morphine, Mark Evans, a Physician's Assistant, said I had at least three heart attacks before this one. He said I should go to the Oklahoma Heart Hospital as soon as possible. But, because there was a bad storm, a helicopter was out of the question, so the ambulance was my next ride. Linda drove along behind us.

When we arrived at the Heart Hospital in Oklahoma City, I was placed on a heart pump after it was determined that I had two 100% blockages, one 98% and one 95%, and the cardiologist was unable to go through any of the arteries.

The only way to deal with the blockages was bypass surgery. However, I was left on a heart pump for three days, giving my heart time to rest as much as possible.

Much of my hospital stay, I do not remember, but I was sure I would not leave the hospital. Linda, my loving wife, was with me all the time I was there. I can remember her rubbing my forehead telling me things were going to be alright. Shannon and Sharra were there as were many other people, although I was in and out most of the time. I know that Shannon was there 10 days.

Doctor John Randolph, probably the best heart surgeon in the area, performed the bypass operation. During the operation, he advised my family I would probably not make it through the surgery, but an hour later, he changed his mind. When he began to plug the bypasses in, the heart began to function normally.

A few days later, I was home. I struggled for several nights and days, unable to lay down or sleep normally, but once the anesthetic was out of my system, I began to do better. Before long, I was walking, eating and, thanks to many people and God, I was going to make it.

Life's Steering Wheel

I know that I would not be here today without Linda, my wife, who initially kept me alive until we reached the hospital. Mark Evans, and the staff at the Oklahoma Heart Hospital, helped me overcome a serious heart attack that would normally have taken my life. In fact, the cardiologist, Todd Lindley and Doctor John Randolph, said they did not understand how I had survived, and they certainly didn't understand why I had no serious damage to my heart.

I know that I have changed in many ways. I look at life more intently, see more beauty in nature, more love for my fellow man. I seem to have less interest in material things. I have lost interest in golf: I am slower to anger and I have no desire to hurt anything, even a skunk, which seems strange. My interest in the guitar has greatly increased as well as my desire to begin writing again.

I am convinced that God chose not to take me from the world at that time. I know that the prayers He heard, made a difference in my life, and I am still trying to understand why he spared my life and what He wants me to do with the remainder of it. Perhaps, I will find the answer, but for now, I try to spend my remaining time with my wife, my children and grandsons, whom I love very much.

If I could offer any worthwhile advise to the readers of this book, it would be to stay close to God, your family and friends. If you maintain these three things in the correct proportion, your life will be enriched and your eternity bright.

Life's Steering Wheel

2685125